Pretty Cross-Stitch for the Home

Pretty Cross-Stitch for the Home

Melinda Coss

MEREDITH® PRESS

For David and Nest Rubio,
both of whom I love dearly

First published in Great Britain in 1994 by
Anaya Publishers Ltd, London

U.S. edition published by
Meredith® Press
150 E. 52nd Street
New York, NY 10022

Meredith® Press is an imprint of Meredith® Books:
President, Book Group: Joseph J. Ward
Vice-President, Editorial Director: Elizabeth P. Rice

Text copyright © Melinda Coss 1994
Photography and illustrations © Anaya Publishers 1994

Managing Editor   Jane Struthers
Design   Peartree Design Associates
Charts and Diagrams   Steve Dew and Delia Elliman
Photography   Di Lewis
Detail photography   J A Ducker

For Meredith® Press:
Executive Editor: Maryanne Bannon
Senior Editor: Carol Spier

All correspondence should be addressed to Meredith® Press.

ISBN 0-696-20275-1
LOC 93-080850

Typeset in Great Britain by Litho Link Ltd, Welshpool, Powys, Wales
Color reproduction by Scantrans Pte Ltd, Singapore
Printed and bound by Dai Nippon in Hong Kong

Distributed by Meredith Corporation, Des Moines, Iowa

This book may not be sold outside the United States of America.

Contents

INTRODUCTION

Our choice in home decoration is influenced by numerous factors. Personal taste, gender, the architecture of the building, the sizes and ages of our families, practicality, expense, fashion, and last but not least, the amount/style of furnishings we need to incorporate from past times and different places all have to be considered.

Faced with finding solutions for all these considerations and having moved nine times in my adult life, the last time I did it I was sorely tempted to leave all the rooms of my new home undecorated and unfurnished as a statement of my personal mobility . . . and would have done so if only I could have handled the trauma of parting with treasured pre-war editions of *Vogue*, rusting milk churns, super-duper, high-tech vegetable chopper-uppers, my children's old school paintings, 45 soft toys all with their own names and stories to tell, and those antique weighing scales that seem to have attached themselves to me over the years.

Then of course there are all those wonderful magazines telling me how rewarding craft work is and that as a homemaker of the 1990s I need to learn how to "distress" my extremely expensive and smooth plaster finishes, how to drape my curtains (what curtains?), and how to turn my milk churn into a piece of art. My beautiful copper pipes should be painted verdigris to make them look as if they are leaking, but while it is highly desirable to own an original cooking range, I really should forget about the coal and

wood and change to oil or gas . . .

My reaction to these mixed messages is "compromise." It is important that my home has individuality and style, but I am not prepared to destroy perfectly good walls to achieve it. If my wood trim

is already curling at the edges, then all well and good – it has accomplished 1990s fashion status all by itself. My leanings, however (and hopefully yours too or you wouldn't be reading this book), are toward needle and thread, and with

needle and thread I will decorate, emphasize, interpret, and enjoy those valuable bits of nostalgia that are now so much a part of me.

If you are making a new home, this book will give you the means to begin your own collection of treasures in cross-stitch. If, like me, your past inspirations travel with you, it is really a question of re-grouping what is in danger of becoming junk and accessorizing it with your cross-stitch skills so that a theme for a particular room becomes apparent and your personal signature is clearly stated. There is no reason on earth why a house should be decorated in one style all over, be it classical or modern. A home should spell out the personalities of the people living

in it and, provided you take color schemes into account, there is no reason why classical and modern decorations cannot work in harmony. If you are comfortable with clutter but have a super-tidy partner, establish space for both: a cozy, cluttered bedroom and a Japanese-style living room could well offer the solution to your problems.

If you have children, use your needle and thread to create environments for them which will not only be individual and stimulating, but will, I guarantee, remain in their memories throughout adulthood.

When you begin to look around your room with a cross-stitcher's eye, numerous items will present

themselves to you for decoration. Those plain curtains, that tablecloth . . . just think carefully and use your skills to coordinate items so that they provide their own overall look.

For cross-stitch beginners, this book will introduce you to a rewarding and therapeutic skill that is easy to master. The techniques section describes a relaxed approach to cross-stitch, and the projects are designed to inspire you with new and interesting ideas that can be worked using almost any of the supplied charts.

Do not feel restricted by my choice of colors – you should select colors that fit in with your own scheme of things. Since recycling is important in this day and age, make use of the bits and pieces around you and use your flair and imagination to give them a new lease on life. If you are making a home on a tight budget, don't spend money on fancy linens and bedding; go for plain colors, which are usually considerably cheaper, and decorate them with cross-stitch.

While my earlier comments might suggest that I am a little bemused by paint finishes that are designed to age your home, I am all in favor of stenciling and freehand painting, both of which can add immense character to a room. You can adapt stencil designs into cross-stitch charts and vice versa, so treat the designs available to you in their broadest possible terms. Just because a chart might be intended for needlepoint, that doesn't mean it can't be used for anything else, and it will probably work beautifully in cross-stitch. Experiment!

I won't keep you any longer because I want you to get started, but one word of warning – cross-stitch is addictive and you might just end up needing to move to a larger house . . .

MELINDA COSS

Page 7: *Spring Bouquet Heart and Little Lace Heart.* Facing page: *Delft Napkin and Delft Tablecloth.* Left: *Japanese Lampshade; Japanese Paperweight; Japanese Sunrise Bookmark; Japanese Address Book; Playing Card Glasses Case; Bridge Pad.* Above: *Cupid on Perforated Paper.*

Kitchens

THE DELFT KITCHEN

There has been a great rise in the popularity of blue and white porcelain and earthenware, and many original pieces are now used decoratively to brighten up a kitchen cupboard. Delftware designs are often chosen for wall tiles because the simple color scheme of cobalt blue on white adds character and charm to a basic kitchen.

Delftware originated in Holland where it served the purpose of "poor man's porcelain." It was, however, a source of grief to the eighteenth-century Dutch housewife since the white tin glaze tended to chip off the underlying clay body. It is ironic to think that many of the domestic items we seek out and treasure today served as a great burden to those who had to use, clean, and care for them in the past.

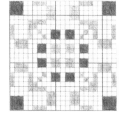

Delft Clock

Kitchen, bathroom, and fireplace tiles provide a wonderful source of inspiration and can easily be translated into attractive cross-stitch designs. The regular shape of the tile and the use of geometric and mirror images makes the motifs suitable for a large number of projects since you can add and remove tile shapes to build up different-sized blocks and borders. For example, in this section, I have made a clock, a tablecoth, a potholder, and a napkin, all based on the designs of Delft tiles. You might choose to make a border for a window shade or to use the square motifs for a picture frame or book cover.

Producing a basic design is simple. You could either trace and chart an image directly from a tile onto graph paper or, if you have a spare tile, you can photocopy it and either enlarge or reduce it to the required size before charting the image on the paper.

Actual design measures:
13 in (33 cm) square

Materials

1 piece of 14-count Aida, in white, measuring approximately 17 in (43 cm) square
No. 7 crewel needle
A piece of masonite or stiff cardboard measuring 13 in (33 cm) square
Rubber-based adhesive
Quartz clock movement and set of hands, with the big hand measuring 3½ in (8.9 cm)
Craft knife

DMC 6-strand embroidery floss:

 4 skeins of light blue (809)

 3 skeins of dark blue (798)

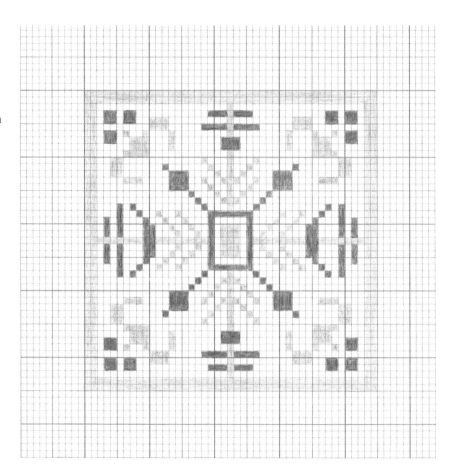

Instructions

I have allowed a 1 inch (2.5 cm) margin at each edge so, if you choose to begin at, say, the bottom right-hand corner, start stitching on the 14th thread in from the right edge and the 14th thread up from the bottom edge and work the outside borders made up from large tiles first. *Note that the tiles are joined horizontally with two rows of stitching instead of four.*

Work the design entirely in cross-stitch, using three strands of floss. Having worked the eight large border motifs, complete the horizontal bands of small motifs and then position the large tile motif that supports the clock hands by finding the center of both the fabric and the chart and working from that point. Finally, position and stitch the numbers for the clock face.

Finishing

When your embroidery is complete, place the fabric right side up squarely on the piece of masonite or cardboard. Fold the margins carefully to the back of the cardboard, turn your work face down, and glue the edges in place, taking care to keep your design square.

With the craft knife, carefully cut the threads in the middle of the center tile so you can insert the clock hand support. If you are using cardboard as a backing, you can make a hole by pushing a knitting needle through this central gap. If you are using masonite, a small hand drill will do the trick. Set the clock works in position following the manufacturer's instructions.

Delft Napkin

To complete the look for your blue-and-white kitchen, you can add a small motif to a set of matching napkins. Position a single motif wherever you choose or work a row of small motifs as a border if you prefer.

Actual design measures:
1½ in (3.8 cm) square

Materials

Cotton and lace trimmed napkin
No. 8 crewel needle
1 piece of 15-count waste canvas,
*   measuring 2½ in (6.3 cm) square*

DMC 6-strand embroidery floss:

 4 skeins of light blue (809)

2 skeins of dark blue (798)

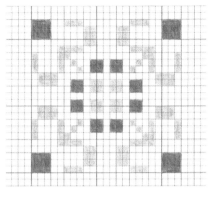

Instructions

Mark the center of the square of waste canvas and baste it into position on your napkins. Using two strands of floss and working over two threads of canvas in cross-stitch throughout, stitch the design. When your embroidery is complete, remove the threads of waste canvas by pulling them from under the stitching with a pair of tweezers.

Delft Tablecloth

Look at auctions and yard sales for old cotton and lace tablecloths, then just by adding a motif here and there, working through waste canvas, you can transform and personalize your finds so they fit in with your room.

The cloth that I have used in this particular project measures 34 inches (86.3 cm) square and is available as a kit (see suppliers information on page 165). Full details of the waste canvas technique are given on page 160.

Actual design measures:
large motif 3¼ in (8.25 cm) square; small motif approximately 1½ in (3.8 cm) square

Materials

1 paneled, lace and cotton tablecloth
*   34 in (86.3 cm) square (see*
*   suppliers information on*
*   page 165)*
No. 8 crewel needle
Contrasting sewing thread for
*   basting*
8 pieces of 15-count waste canvas
*   measuring 4 in (10 cm) square*
8 pieces of 15-count waste canvas
*   measuring 2½ in (6.3 cm) square*
Pair of tweezers

DMC 6-strand embroidery floss:

4 skeins of light blue (809)

2 skeins of dark blue (798)

Instructions

First mark the center point of each square of waste canvas. Using plain sewing thread, baste the squares of waste canvas onto the woven cotton squares of the tablecloth, positioning them alternately, one large then one small, along the rows until all 16 woven squares of cloth are covered.

Using two strands of floss and working in cross-stitch throughout over two threads of canvas, start at the center of your chart and work each motif in turn, taking care to ensure that all the stitches cross in the same direction (you will notice that the squares lie at an angle on the cloth to form diamond images).

When you have completed the embroidery, use tweezers to pull out the threads of waste canvas carefully from under the stitching.

Delft Potholder

This clever little potholder was purchased complete with Aida panel (see suppliers information on page 165). You can, however, make your own very easily and decorate it with a combination of the tile motifs. For my potholder I have used two of the large motifs from page 14 side by side, but you could use four small motifs, one at each corner, or a border of small motifs across the middle of the panel.

Actual design measures:
6½ × 3¼ in (16.5 × 8.25 cm)

Materials
1 piece of 14-count Aida in ecru measuring 6½ × 7½ in (6.5 × 19 cm)
No. 7 crewel needle
2 pieces of terrycloth measuring 8 in (20.5 cm) square
Sewing thread in a matching color
1 piece of polyester batting measuring 8 in (20cm) square
1¾ yards (1.5 meters) of 1-in (2.5-cm) wide bias tape to trim

DMC 6-strand embroidery floss:

 1 skein of dark blue (798)

1 skein of light blue (809)

Instructions
Find the center of the Aida and the central point of the double tile chart and begin stitching here. Using three strands of floss and cross-stitch throughout, work the two large tiles side by side as indicated on the chart.

When the embroidery is complete, set the Aida to one side and sandwich the batting between the two squares of terrycloth.

Finishing
My purchased potholder has been quilted by machine with diagonal lines of straight stitching. If you do not have a sewing machine, simply sew the three layers of fabric together using a row of backstitch approximately ½ inch (12 mm) from the edge of the fabric. You could quilt the fabric by hand if you are unable to find anything suitable that is ready-quilted.

Cut a length of bias tape measuring 7½ inches (19 cm) long, fold this over the top edge of your worked Aida and sew it in place. Carefully lay your Aida right side up on top of your padded square of terrycloth, lining up the bottom edges. Baste into position along the side and bottom edges. Fold the remaining bias tape in half and, starting center bottom, fold and pin it into position over the raw edges of fabric, leaving two loose ends at the center top. Using backstitch, or better still a sewing machine, stitch the bias tape securely into position. Cross the loose ends at the top and join neatly to form a loop for hanging.

THE
STRAWBERRY
KITCHEN

Wild strawberries always remind me of vacations spent in the mountains of France, so I have used this motif to accessorize a Provençal kitchen. Summer fruits of all kinds are popular embroidery motifs, and in traditional samplers a basket of fruit is said to symbolize fertility. In view of this, and just to be on the safe side. I have left out the baskets since the prospect of a band of pregnant cross-stitchers beating down my publisher's door is more than I can bear. Instead, I have used strawberry motifs of various styles and presented them within a mini-sampler, complete with alphabet.

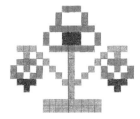

Strawberry Sampler Pillow

Using the waste-canvas technique, this embroidery is cross-stitched onto a ready-made cotton and lace pillow cover. Pillow covers of this style are easy to come by both through the major stores and in antique markets and auctions. When hunting for cottons and linens to embroider, try to select those incorporating plain fabric panels and let the shape of the panel suggest a design or the positioning of a design to you.

Creating a sampler is always an interesting exploration of a motif since you can use a single image in many different ways, each of which may illustrate a mood or overall style for a piece of work. Experiment by working the same motif in different threads and on different backgrounds and then join your working samples together into a patchwork. Depending on size, this could then be transformed into a wallhanging or a book cover, or anything else that you feel might prove useful and attractive within your room.

Actual design measures:
4¾ × 5 in (12 × 12.7 cm)

Materials

Cotton and lace pillow cover measuring 16 in (40.6 cm) square (see suppliers information on page 165)
Contrasting sewing thread for basting
No. 8 crewel needle
1 piece of 15-count waste canvas measuring 5½ in (14 cm) square
Pair of tweezers

DMC 6-strand embroidery floss:

1 skein of pink (893)
1 skein of rose (956)
1 skein of green (3348)
1 skein of light pink (3708)

Instructions

Mark the center point of your waste canvas. Baste the waste canvas onto the central panel of the pillow cover with contrasting sewing thread.

Mark the center of the chart and work from here, in cross-stitch, using two strands of floss and working over two threads of canvas. Please note that the design fits very snugly on central panel, so be very careful to center the work correctly. The double-check this, I suggest that you work the motif closest to the center and then count outward to the border so you can see exactly where it is positioned.

When you have completed the embroidery, gently pull out the waste canvas threads from under the stitching with the tweezers.

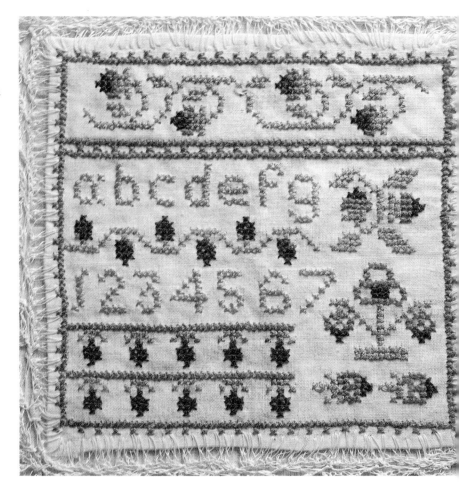

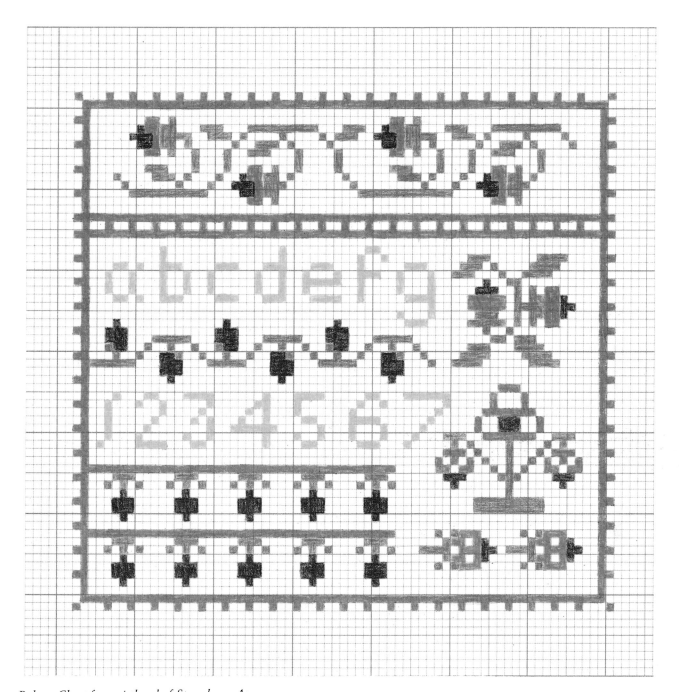

Below: Chart for waistband of Strawberry Apron

Strawberry Apron

For this project I have used the repeat motif at the top of the sampler to work a waistband for a pretty lace and cotton apron. I have also added interest by framing a single motif and using it as a patch on the pocket. The apron I used was purchased and is available by mail order (see suppliers information on page 165). You can of course use the same chart for a waistband on a skirt or select a single motif and use it on the collar or pocket of a shirt. The waistband chart (see bottom of page 21) can be repeated to whatever length you wish and would also look pretty as a trimming for a window shade or as a border for a plain pillow. If you have bench seating in your kitchen, why not make a long cushion to fit it and edge it with a strawberry border?

Actual designs measure:
waistband design area
1 × 13 in (2.5 × 33 cm);
pocket design area
1¾ × 2 in (4.5 × 5 cm)

Materials
Lace and cotton apron, available by mail order (see suppliers information on page 165)
No. 8 crewel needle
1 strip of 15-count waste canvas to fit the design area on the waistband plus 1 in (2.5 cm) extra – e.g. 2 × 14 in (5 × 35.5 cm)
1 piece of 15-count waste canvas measuring 3 in (7.5 cm) square
Pair of tweezers

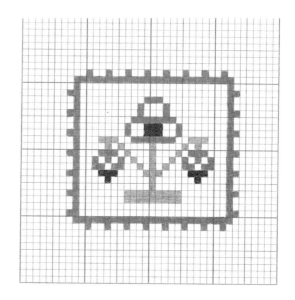

DMC 6-strand embroidery floss:

 1 skein of pink (893)

 1 skein of rose (956)

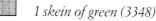 *1 skein of green (3348)*

Instructions
Baste the waste canvas into position, centering it on the waistband. Center and baste the 3-inch (7.5-cm) square of canvas to the pocket front.

Waistband Mark the center of the waistband and the center of the 62-stitch pattern repeat on the chart, i.e. stitch 31. Begin reading the chart from the center, working in cross-stitch with two strands of floss over two threads of canvas. Work from the center of the chart back to the left edge and then repeat the complete 62-stitch chart, reading it from right to left. Return to the center, complete reading the second half of the chart from left to right, then repeat the whole 62-stitch chart, reading it from left to right. With tweezers, carefully pull out the threads of waste canvas from under the finished embroidery.

Pocket Mark the center of the waste canvas on the pocket and the center of the design on the chart. Work the entire motif in cross-stitch using two strands of floss over two threads of canvas. When the embroidery is complete, carefully pull out the threads of waste canvas from under the finished stitching.

Strawberry Jam Pots

Homemade preserves taste delicious, look delicious, and make very welcome gifts. These little jam pot covers are available complete with their own Aida panels, ready for you to add the embroidery. If you prefer, you can make your own by cutting out a circle of Aida to the size of your jam pot lid and adding a lace trim around the edge.

Actual designs measure:
1½ × 1¾ in (3.8 × 4.5 cm) and
1½ in (3.8 cm) square

Materials
2 lace-trimmed jam pot lids or two circles of 18-count Aida measuring approximately 3 in (7.5 cm) in diameter
1¼ yards (1 meter) of 2-in (5-cm) wide lace trim
No. 8 crewel needle
Sewing thread to match the lace
Pencil
Narrow ribbon to trim

DMC 6-strand embroidery floss:

 1 skein pink (893)

 1 skein rose (956)

 1 skein green (3348)

Instructions
Mark the center of the Aida band and the center of the chart. If you are using purchased lids simply work from the center point in cross stitch using two strands of floss. If you are making the pot covers yourself, place the lid you intend to cover on the Aida and draw a circle in pencil around it. With sewing thread, overcast the edge in zigzag stitch to avoid fraying. Cut your length of lace in half and gather along one long edge, then stitch it carefully to the Aida circle. Tie covers over jars with ribbon.

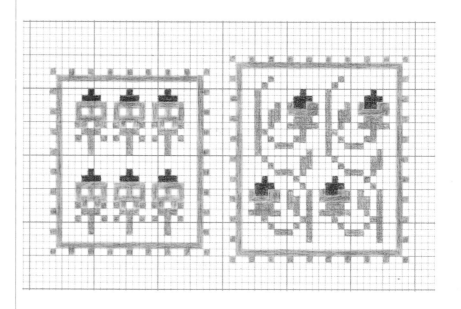

CHICKEN-AND-FISH STEW KITCHEN

I am lucky enough to occupy a design studio that overlooks a meadow, and I have among my constant companions four very fat hens who range free in front of my window. Through the other window there is a stream where, on a good day, one can find an exhausted salmon who has swum a very long way in order to get here. For this reason, I always associate country kitchens with chickens and fish and, since I am based in Wales, leeks are also a part of the picture.

A sampler is traditionally a practice piece worked in an assortment of stitches and illustrated with a number of different motifs. Why not select a collection of motifs that are meaningful to you and your family and incorporate them into your kitchen cross-stitching. Samplers are informal pieces, and to my mind, the designs on them should be placed at random surrounding one central panel. If you are design-shy, you can do as I have done and repeat the same motif to form a row, or work it as a series of mirror images.

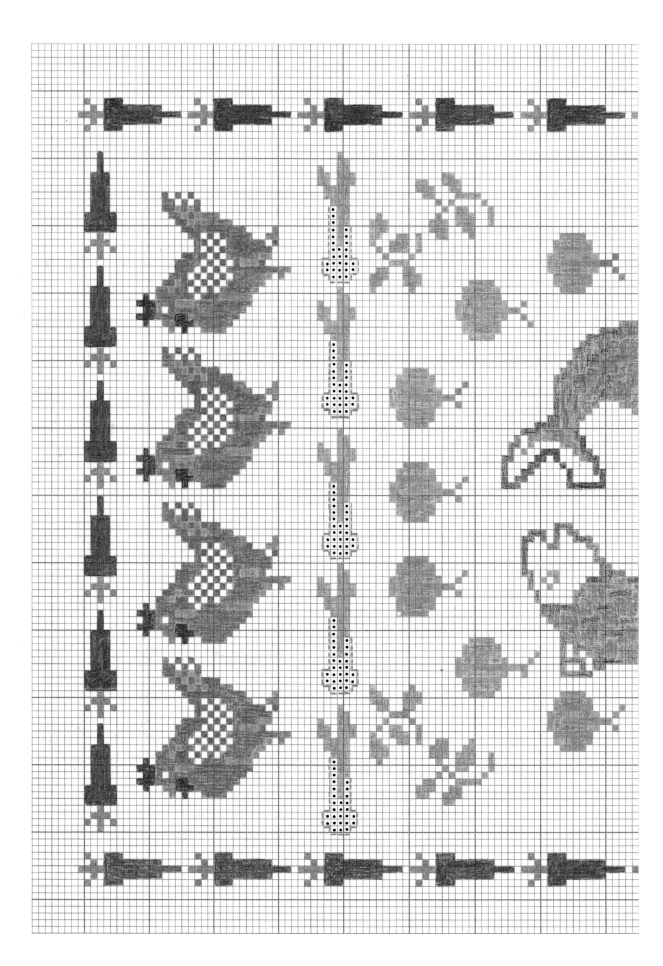

Chicken-and-Fish Stew Sampler

I have chosen to frame this piece and hang it on a wall, but it could also be used as the front cover for a binder or scrapbook to keep your recipes in. You will find instructions for making a folder in the Noah's Ark children's room section (see page 61).

Actual design measurements:
8¾ × 12½ in (22.25 × 31.75 cm)

Materials
1 piece of 14-count Aida measuring
*   12 × 15 in (30.5 × 38 cm)*
No. 24 tapestry needle

The chart for the Chicken-and-Fish
Stew Sampler is shown on pages 28–9.

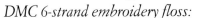

DMC 6-strand embroidery floss:

- *2 skeins of orange (970)*
- *2 skeins of rust (900)*
- *1 skein of caramel (437)*
- *1 skein of orange (741)*
- *1 skein of green (912)*
- *1 skein of white*
- *1 skein of coral (351)*
- *1 skein of khaki (611)*
- *1 skein of red (606)*

Instructions
Mark the center of the chart and the center of the Aida. Starting here, work in cross-stitch using three strands of floss. When the embroidery is complete, frame it according to your taste.

Fish Runner

Table runners are coming back into fashion and have never lost their popularity in mid-European countries. A Norwegian friend tells me that she has a complete set of embroidered table linens to cover every season, so her kitchen welcomes the spring with linens embroidered in green and yellows and provides a cozy setting for winter with red and green embroideries. She also has runners and napkins for special occasions such as Christmas and Easter, so she knows her table will always look fresh and festive.

Actual design measures:
3½ × 4¾ in (8.9 × 12 cm)

Materials
No. 8 crewel needle
Pins
Sewing thread for basting
1 piece of 34-count linen, hemmed
*   to measure 8 × 34½ in*
*   (20.5 × 86.8 cm)*

DMC 6-strand embroidery floss:

- *1 skein of coral (351)*
- *2 skeins of khaki (611)*
- *1 skein of green (912)*

Instructions

Place a pin 2 inches (5 cm) in from both sides of runner and stitch a row of basting from top to bottom at both ends. Place another pair of pins 2 inches (5 cm) in from both the long edges of the runner and stitch two more rows of basting top and bottom, the length of the runner. Find the center right-hand edge of the chart and the center of the right-hand vertical row of basting and start here, working in cross-stitch using two strands of floss over two threads of linen. When the first block of fishes is complete, work the left-hand block of fishes, positioning them in the same way. Fold the runner in half horizontally and mark the center. Mark the center of the chart and begin the middle block of fishes here. Work in cross-stitch throughout until the embroidery is complete.

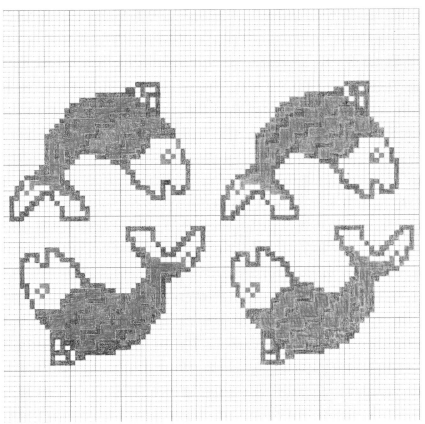

The fish chart can be used for both the salt box and a table runner.

Chicken-and-Fish Salt Box

Squares of embroidered fabric can be used to decorate useful boxes of all kinds. Here I have used a whitewood salt box that I bought from a general store with the idea of keeping bouillion cubes in it – chicken for chicken, fish for fish, and so on. Work whichever panel suits your purpose.

Actual designs measure:
Chicken panel 2¾ in × 3¼ in
(7 × 8.25 cm)
Fish panel 2¾ × 3¾ in
(7 × 9.5 cm)

Materials

*1 square of 14-count Aida measuring
    6 in (15.25 cm) for each panel
1 piece of cardboard cut to fit each
    panel you intend covering
1 piece of polyester batting the same
    size as the cardboard
No. 24 tapestry needle
Rubber-based adhesive*

FOR THE CHICKEN PANEL
DMC 6-strand embroidery floss:

- 1 skein of green (912)
- 1 skein of red (606)
- 1 skein of caramel (437)
- 1 skein of orange (741)
- 1 skein of rust (900)

FOR THE FISH PANEL
DMC 6-strand embroidery floss:

- 1 skein of khaki (611)
- 1 skein of green (912)
- 1 skein of coral (351)

Instructions

Mark the center of the selected chart and the center of the Aida. Starting here, work in cross-stitch using three strands of floss until the design is complete. Cut out the cardboard to fit the box front and glue the batting on top of the cardboard. Center the panel of embroidery over the batting, wrap and glue the edges to the back of the cardboard. Glue the mounted panels securely into position on the box and leave to dry.

Chicken Basket Liner

I have used an odd, scallop-edged napkin to make this lining for a basket of eggs. You could choose to use a cheerful square of gingham or tartan fabric or simply hem the edges of a piece of sheeting for the same effect.

If you have drawn your own motif and wish to increase its size, redraw it on graph paper, drawing four symbols for every one symbol on your original. When your design is complete, you may want to round off the edges by rubbing out a few stitches here and there.

Actual design measures:
$3 \times 3\frac{1}{2}$ in (7.5 × 8.9 cm)

Materials

1 white cotton napkin
1 piece of 15-count waste canvas
measuring 5 in (12.7 cm) square
No. 8 crewel needle
Sewing thread for basting
Pair of tweezers

DMC 6-strand embroidery floss:

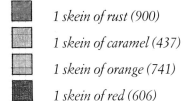

1 skein of rust (900)

1 skein of caramel (437)

1 skein of orange (741)

1 skein of red (606)

Instructions

Baste the waste canvas in position across one corner of the napkin. Mark the center of the chart and the center of the waste canvas and start here, working in cross-stitch using two strands of floss over two threads of canvas. Work until the embroidery is complete. With tweezers, carefully remove the waste canvas from under the stitching.

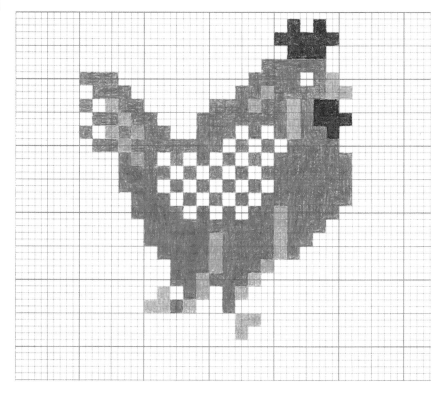

Nurseries

DUCKS, RABBITS, AND MICE NURSERY

Baby animals of all sorts are popular friends in a baby's room and can be featured in numerous ways. Outlines from these cuddly characters can be traced and made into stencils to create painted borders and motifs on walls, cupboards, and cribs, or the single panels can be embroidered and framed as pictures in their own right. Use these motifs for birthday cards or embroider a row of ducks along the bottom of a little girl's dress – the possibilities are endless. Here are four ideas that I've come up with to get you started.

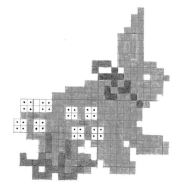

Ducks, Rabbits, and Mice Patchwork Quilt

This pretty quilt can be made in no end of color combinations. I have chosen to work the embroideries on pink Aida surrounded by traditional floral fabrics. You could achieve a fresh look by placing the embroideries among single-colored striped, dotted, and gingham fabrics or, if you are an experienced quilter, you could quilt intricate panels on plain fabric and slot in the animals as and where you choose. Experiment with graph paper, drawing a layout, and positioning the motifs in different ways. Produce more or fewer motif squares as you wish or work the designs on a white background and trim the quilt with eyelet lace. The following instructions are for the quilt you see in the photograph.

Actual design measures:
area of each chart is 4 × 4½ ins (10 × 11.5 cm)
Finished quilt measures 29½ × 40½ ins (75 × 102.87 cm)

Materials

6 pieces of 14-count Aida each measuring 6 in (15.25 cm) square
12 pieces of pale blue, 9 pieces of yellow and 8 pieces of pink lightweight cotton print fabric each measuring 6 in (15.25 cm) square
1 piece of cotton print for backing and border measuring 32 × 45 in (81 × 114 cm)
1 piece of polyester batting measuring 29½ × 40½ in (75 × 102.87 cm)
White sewing thread
No. 8 crewel needle

TO MAKE 2 DUCK SQUARES
DMC 6-strand embroidery floss:

2 skeins of aqua (519)
1 skein of white
1 skein of blue (340)
1 skein of pink (956)
1 skein of turquoise (518)
2 skeins of yellow (727)
1 skein of orange (741)
1 skein of black (310) (eye)
1 skein of dark yellow (725)

TO MAKE 2 MICE SQUARES
DMC 6-strand embroidery floss:

1 skein of fawn (841)
1 skein of camel (437)
1 skein of black (310)
1 skein of white
2 skeins of aqua (519)
1 skein of yellow (727)
1 skein of blue (340)
1 skein of pink (956)
1 skein of mauve (210)

TO MAKE 2 RABBIT SQUARES
DMC 6-strand embroidery floss:

1 skein of gray (45)
1 skein of white
1 skein of pink (956)
2 skeins of aqua (519)
1 skein of yellow (727)
1 skein of blue (340)
1 skein of camel (437)
1 skein of green (3347)

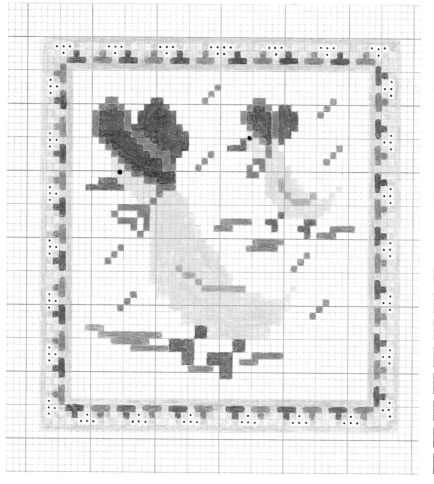

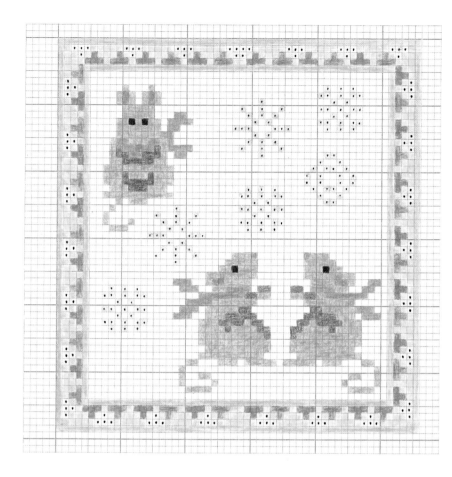

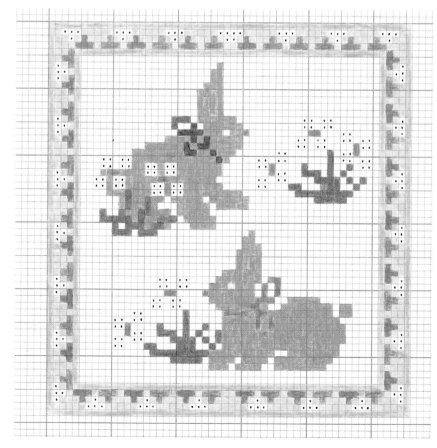

Instructions

Mark the center of the charts and the center of the Aida. Using three strands of floss, work the designs in cross-stitch starting here and following the charts. When the embroidery is complete, press with a warm iron, laying the completed embroidery right side down over a towel. Pin the squares together in vertical strips, positioning them as the layouts show. Machine stitch or hand sew the squares of each strip together, using ¼ inch (6 cm) seam allowance. When you have completed the five strips of squares, join them vertically. Press ¼ inch (6 mm) to the wrong side along all sides.

Lay your backing fabric wrong side up. Place the batting on top and center the patchwork, right side up, on top of the batting. Fold the backing fabric over the batting and tuck behind the patchwork edges. Pin the layers of fabric together and carefully machine stitch with a straight stitch around the edges of the patchwork top, catching the backing into position.

The layout for the Ducks, Rabbits, and Mice Patchwork Quilt is shown on page 42.

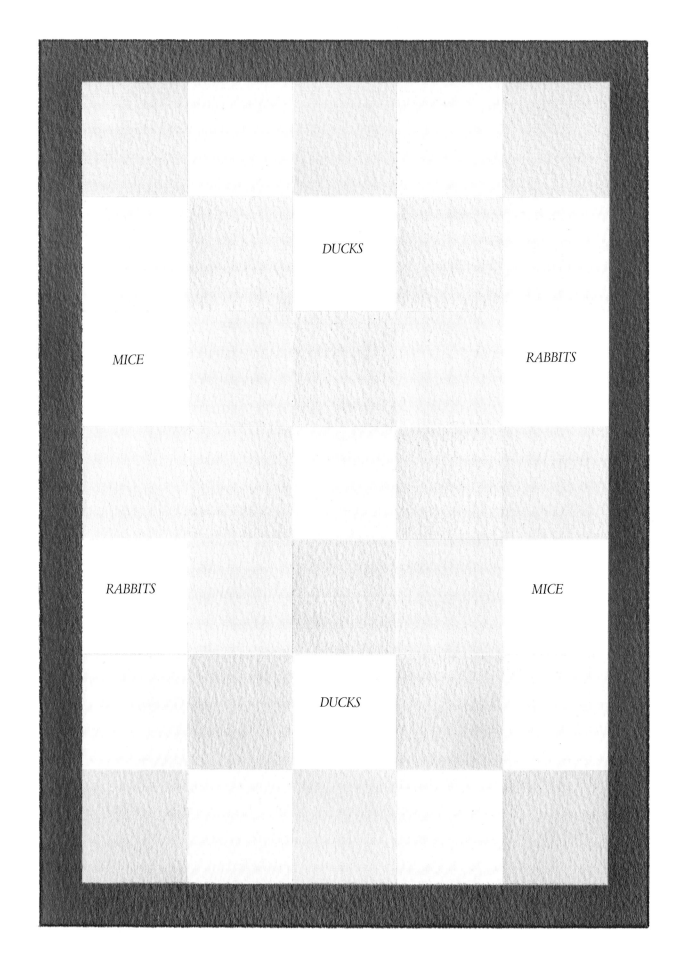

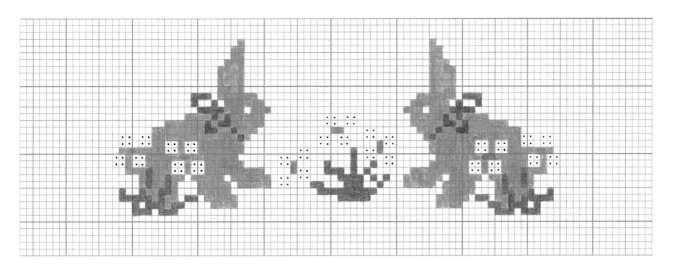

Rabbit Bib

Add these rabbits to an inexpensive terrycloth bib to turn it into something special. You could also repeat this pattern to make a border of rabbits on a child's skirt or along a nursery shade or curtain. Alter the colors of the rabbits and the flowers to add interest.

Actual design measures:
2 × 5 in (5 × 12.7 cm)

Materials

1 terrycloth bib
1 piece of 14-count Aida measuring
  7½ in (19 cm) – or 1 in (2.5 cm)
  wider than the actual bib –
  × 3 in (7.5 cm)
2 lengths of ½-in (12-mm) wide
  satin ribbon, each 1 in (2.5 cm)
  longer than the actual bib
No. 8 crewel needle

DMC 6-strand embroidery floss:

- 1 skein of gray (45)
- 1 skein of camel (437)
- 1 skein of blue (340)
- 1 skein of green (3347)
- 1 skein of pink (956)
- 1 skein of white

Instructions

Mark the center of the chart and the center of the Aida. Work in cross-stitch from here, using three strands of floss. When the embroidery is complete, fold under the short ends of the Aida and stitch into position across the bib. Pin lengths of ribbon along the top and bottom edges of the Aida. Hand sew or machine stitch in place.

Mice Nursery Bag

Taking a new baby out with you feels almost like moving house, there are so many bits of paraphernalia that have to travel with you, and how do you carry them? This smart bag could hold all your disposable diapers, bottles, and toys, and the handle allows you to hang it on your stroller without trailing on the ground.

Actual design measures:
8¾ × 10¾ in (22.25 × 27.5 cm)

Materials

1 piece of 11-count ecru Aida measuring 12½ in (31.25 cm) square
1 piece of heavyweight cotton tweed fabric measuring 20 × 44 in (51 × 111.75 cm)
1¼ yards (1 meter) of 1-in (2.5-cm) wide webbing for the handle
2 wooden toggle beads
1 spool of Kreinik Ombre Silver 1000
No. 8 crewel needle

DMC 6-strand embroidery floss:

1 skein of fawn (841)

2 skeins of camel (437)

1 skein of yellow (727)

1 skein of blue (340)

1 skein of black (310)

1 skein of mauve (210)

3 skeins of aqua (519)

2 skeins of pink (956)

1 skein of white

1 skein of aqua (519) plus Kreinik Silver (see above)

Instructions

Mark the center of the chart and the center of the Aida. Work in cross-stitch from here using four strands of floss, with the exception of the snowflakes, which are worked with one strand of silver thread and one strand of aqua (519) floss. When the embroidery is complete, fold back the excess Aida and baste, leaving a plain border measuring approximately ¾ inch (19 mm).

Finishing

Lay out the cotton fabric and fold the top and bottom (short ends) to form a hem 2½ inches (6.3 cm) deep; hand sew or machine stitch in place. Fold the fabric in half, position the embroidered panel in the center of the front half, and stitch in place around the edges. Fold the fabric in half with right sides facing and sew the side seams. Turn right side out. Thread the webbing through the toggle beads and knot securely. Stitch the webbing to the top of the bag just above the toggle beads, positioning the ends over the side seams.

The chart for the Mice Nursery Bag is shown on pages 46–7; the key is on page 45.

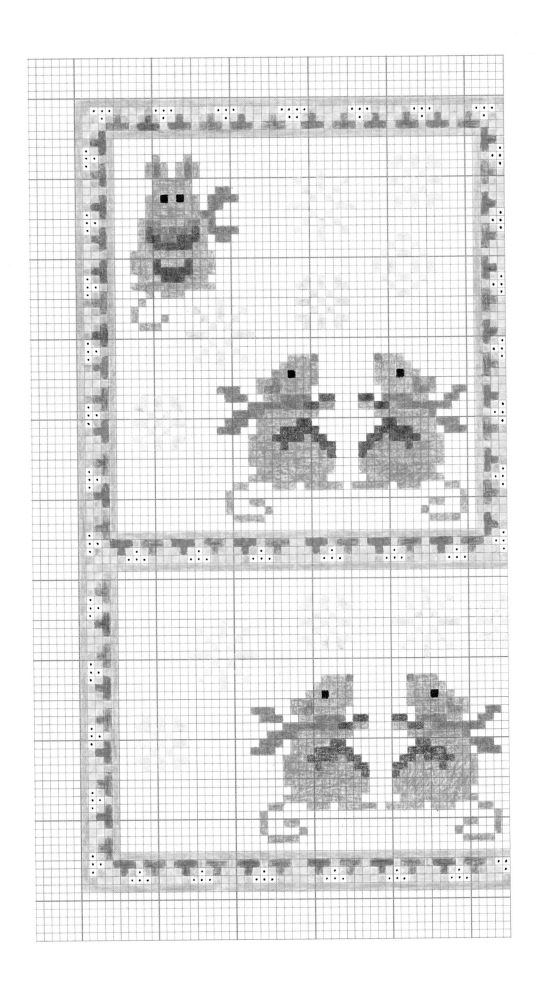

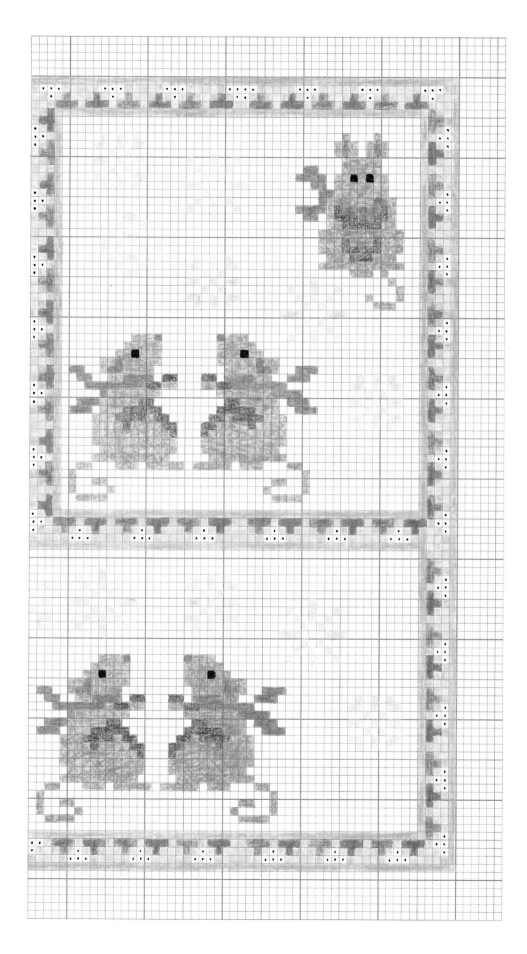

Duck Pillowcase Trim

Decorate a plain nursery pillow with ducks. You can repeat the baby ducks as many times as you wish or just work the mother duck on her own. If you wish, you could repeat the border right around the pillowcase – it all depends on how much work you feel like putting into the project. Or why not work the ducks as a yoke across a baby's dress? This design is worked using the waste-canvas method, for which full directions can be found on page 160.

Actual design (ducks only) measures:
3 × 7 in (7.5 × 17.8 cm)

Materials

Cotton pillowcase trimmed with eyelet lace, measuring approximately 13 × 17½ in (33 × 44.5 cm)
1 piece of 15-count waste canvas measuring 6 in (15.25 cm) wide × the edge of the pillowcase
Contrasting sewing thread for basting
No. 7 crewel needle
Pair of tweezers

DMC 6-strand embroidery floss:

1 skein of aqua (519)
1 skein of white
1 skein of blue (340)
1 skein of pink (956)
1 skein of turquoise (518)
1 skein of yellow (727)
1 skein of orange (741)
1 skein of black (310) (eye)
1 skein of dark yellow (725)

Instructions

Baste the waste canvas into the desired position on the pillowcase. Work the bottom border first, using two strands of floss in cross-stitch throughout. Work the ducks, starting with the mother and adding as many little ones as you wish. Work them in cross-stitch with the exception of the eyes, which are worked as small black straight stitches. When the ducks are complete, work the top border. When the embroidery is complete, carefully remove the waste canvas from under your stitching with tweezers.

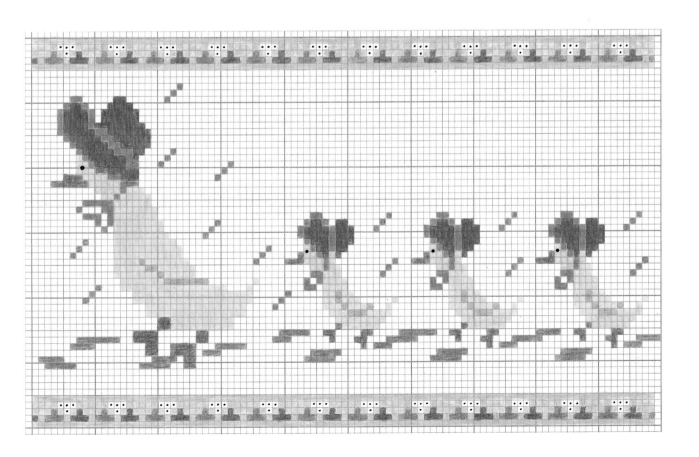

CLOWNS, STARS, AND NUMBERS PLAYROOM

Clowns and stars in primary colors will brighten up a child's playroom and be popular with both boys and girls. Add some numbers or letters, and learning will become a matter of fun.

Clowns can be used in lots of ways. You can stitch them on Herta, cut them to shape, and back them in felt to make cuddly soft toys. Frame them individually, stitch them on perforated paper to use as a mobile, or even cross-stitch one on a sweatshirt.

For very young kids, why not make your own set of blocks using the stars and numbers charts. Work six equal-sized squares of Herta, using a different number or star on each one, and stitch them together over a foam block to form a soft, washable block. Here are some other ideas for you.

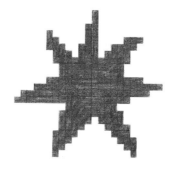

Clown Bag

This jolly bag is very easy to make and could be used for laundry, shoes, toys, or anything else that is best hidden away in a bag. I have used a simple drawstring opening, but you could cut the front panel 8 inches (20.5 cm) shorter than the back panel and fold over the back panel to form a flap which could be fastened to the front with buttons. Add two straps to the back and you have a backpack or school bag. The following instructions are to make the bag that has been photographed.

Actual design measures:
5 × 15 in (12.7 × 38 cm)

Materials

1 piece of 11-count Aida measuring 7 × 18 in (17.8 × 45.7 cm)
2 pieces of heavyweight red cotton fabric each measuring 20 × 30 in (50.8 × 76.2 cm)
2¾ yards (2½ meters) of white cord
Sewing thread to match the backing
No. 23 tapestry needle
2 beads

DMC 6-strand embroidery floss:

1 skein of yellow (725)
1 skein of turquoise (995)
1 skein of mauve (552)
1 skein of orange (741)
1 skein of red (606)
1 skein of black (310)
1 skein of green (701)
1 skein of pale beige (224)

Instructions

Mark the center of the chart and the center of the Aida. Starting here, work in cross-stitch using four strands of floss. When the embroidery is complete, center the panel across the bottom of one piece of the heavyweight cotton fabric approximately 1½ inches (3.8 cm) from the bottom and side edges, allowing an additional ¾ inch (19 mm) of the cotton for seams. Machine sew or backstitch into position, turning under

approximately ¾ inch (19 mm) of the Aida at the edges. When the embroidery is stitched into position, fold under the top of the red fabric to create a casing 2 inches (5 cm) deep through which to thread your cord. Take the second piece of cotton fabric and finish the top to match. Place the two pieces of fabric right sides together and machine sew or backstitch the side and bottom seams. Turn right side out. Cut the length of cord in half and thread one piece through the top back casing and one piece through the top front casing. Thread the ends of the cord through one bead on each edge and knot to secure.

Juggling Stars

Everybody is juggling. It is therapeutic, relaxing, and helps to improve your coordination. Make these juggling balls from scraps of fabric and decorate them with cross-stitch stars or numbers. Fill them with lentils or dried beans.

Actual design measures: approximately 2 in (5 cm) square

Materials
3 pieces of 11-count Aida, each measuring 4 in (10 cm) square
1 piece of silver lurex or felt measuring 6 × 31½ in (15.25 × 80 cm)
14 oz (400 g) lentils or dried beans
Sewing thread to match fabric
No. 23 tapestry needle

DMC 6-strand embroidery floss:

1 skein of red (606)

1 skein of turquoise (995)

1 skein of green (701)

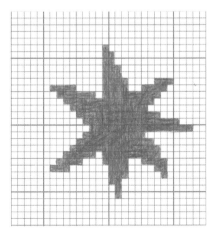

Instructions
Mark the center of the charts and the center of the Aida. Staring here, work in cross-stitch using four strands of floss to complete the three star panels. Cut out six circles approximately 4½ inches (11.5 cm) in diameter (use a jar top as a

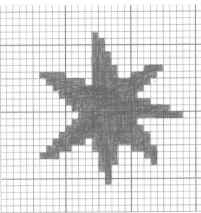

template) from the silver fabric or felt. Center the squares of embroidered Aida on three of the circles of fabric and backstitch into position, turning under the edges of the Aida so the finished panels are approximately 2½ inches (6.3 cm) square. Place each of the three

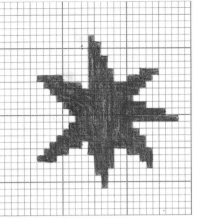

remaining circles of fabric right sides together over an embroidered circle. Stitch firmly around the edges leaving a 2-inch (5-cm) gap. Turn the circles right side out and fill with the lentils or dried beans. Firmly stitch the openings closed.

Clown Card

Children love receiving personalized greeting cards. You can insert the correct age using the number chart, so you could adapt this design for significant birthdays for adults.

Actual design measures:
4½ in (11.5 cm) square

Materials

1 piece of 14-count Aida measuring
  6 × 7 in (15.25 × 17.8 cm)
1 piece of cardboard measuring
  8¼ × 17½ in (21 × 43.5 cm)
No. 24 tapestry needle
Craft knife
Rubber-based adhesive

DMC 6-strand embroidery floss:

1 skein of yellow (725)
1 skein of turquoise (995)
1 skein of mauve (552)
1 skein of red (606)
1 skein of green (701)
1 skein of pale beige (224)
1 skein of black (310)

Instructions

Mark the center of the chart and the center of the Aida. Starting here, work the design in cross-stitch using three strands of floss. Fold the card into three equal parts crosswise. Cut a rectangle in the center panel to fit the embroidery. Glue the finished embroidery on the center of the left-hand panel. Apply glue to the border of the cutout area on the center panel, tuck the embroidered piece behind it and press down.

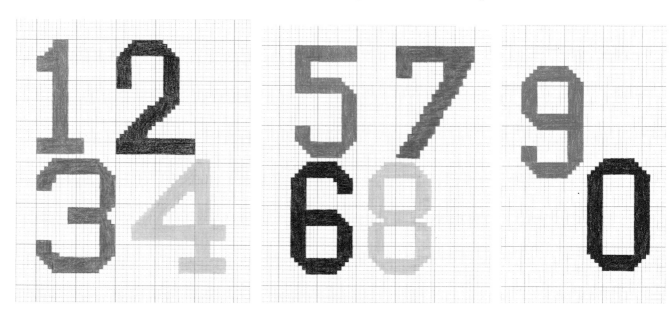

Clown Grow Chart

Use this fun chart to keep track of how the children are growing. The sliding flags will help you to identify who has reached which height and means you won't have to make marks on your walls.

Materials

1 piece of 14-count Aida measuring
*   6½ × 43 in (16.5 × 109.25 cm)*
1 piece of white sheeting measuring
*   6½ × 43 in (16.5 × 109.25 cm)*
1 length of 1-in (2.5-cm) wide ribbon
*   measuring 62 in (157.5 cm) long*
White sewing thread
No. 25 tapestry needle
A tape measure
3 heavy beads or weights
8-in (20.5-cm) batten or stick for
*   hanging*
Rubber-based adhesive
Colored posterboard

DMC 6-strand embroidery floss:

1 skein of yellow (725)

2 skeins of turquoise (995)

2 skeins of mauve (552)

1 skein of red (606)

1 skein of black (310)

1 skein of green (701)

1 skein of pale peach (224)

1 skein of orange (741)

Instructions

Allowing ½ inch (12 mm) margin at each edge, count up from the bottom of the Aida piece to find the position of the first turquoise star. Starting here, begin following the chart in cross-stitch, using two strands of floss throughout. Work the straight stitch detail in black, using two strands of floss.

Finishing

Place the completed embroidery on top of the strip of sheeting and turn under and pin ½ inch (12 mm) on all edges. Stitch the edges, leaving a 1-inch (2.5-cm) gap at the top of both side seams for the batten. With the ribbon, make a loop at the top for the batten. Cut the bottom so that the ribbon is the same length as the chart. Cut the bottom 19½ inches (49.5 cm) off of the tape measure. Glue the remainder to the length of ribbon. Make flags with your children's names by cutting circles from the posterboard and making two horizontal slits, approximately 1 inch (2.5 cm) apart and 1 inch (2.5 cm) wide in each one. Write your child's name above the top slit. Slide these flags onto the ribbon. Loop the tape measure over the batten to hang beside your completed growth chart. Tie one bead or weight at each bottom corner of the chart and one at the bottom of the tape. Hang the completed chart 19½ inches (49.5 cm) above the floor.

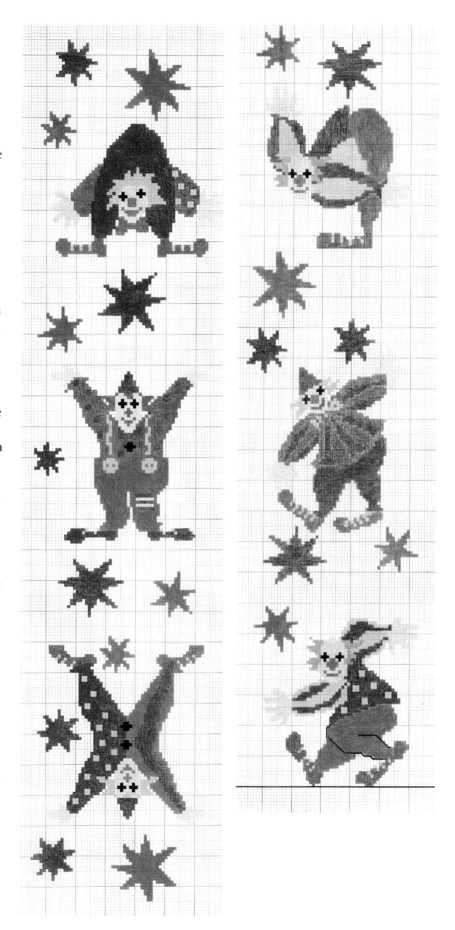

NOAH'S ARK
CHILDREN'S ROOM

Do you remember starting school and wanting your very own desk to study on at home? This group of designs is especially for kids who are beginning to take an interest in their surroundings and treasuring all those things that make school times interesting. The story is an old one . . . Mr. and Mrs. Noah and their followers saving the world with their Ark. You can mix and match the animals as you choose (provided you keep them in twos) or you could use different motifs that reflect the child's hobbies or interests or encourage them to produce cross-stitch panels of their own which you could make into interesting schooltime assessories. The possibilities are endless.

Ark Folder

If you have some leftover curtain fabric or even wallpaper, you could make this folder, which can be used as a scrapbook, a collector's album, or simply a project folder. I have used cotton ticking, but any medium-weight fabric would do.

Actual design measures:
9 × 13¼ in (22.9 × 33.6 cm)

Materials

1 piece of 11-count Aida measuring 12 × 17 in (30.5 × 43 cm)
2 pieces of cotton ticking each measuring 17 × 22 in (43 × 56 cm)
2 pieces of red felt, each measuring 12 × 17 in (30.5 × 43 cm)
2¼ yards (2 meters) yarn, ribbon, or tape for ties
1¼ yards (1 meter) ½-in (12-mm) wide ribbon to hold paper
2 pieces of stiff cardboard, each measuring 13½ × 18½ in (34.25 × 47 cm)
Sheet of paper measuring 11½ × 16 in (29 × 42 cm)
Small rectangle of posterboard
Rubber-based adhesive
White sewing thread
No. 8 crewel needle
Hole punch
Pencil

DMC 6-strand embroidery floss:

1 skein of black (310)
1 skein of gray (45)
1 skein of fawn (437)
1 skein of yellow (444)
2 skeins of blue (798)
1 skein of aqua (518)
1 skein of red (606)
1 skein of brown (632)
1 skein of pale peach (3779)
1 skein of turquoise (995)
1 skein of lime (834)
1 skein of green (906)
1 skein of pink (223)
1 skein of white
1 skein of greenish blue (954)

Instructions

Mark the center of the chart and the center of the Aida, and work from here in cross-stitch using three strands of floss and adding the final straight stitch detail in colors as indicated on the key by the chart.

Cover the back of one piece of cardboard with ticking; fold the excess to the other side and glue down. Using this back cover as a guide, pin the sampler to the center of the remaining piece of ticking, folding under the edges so you have a plain ½-inch (12 mm) border of Aida all around your picture. Stitch this into position over the ticking and use it to cover the remaining piece of board.

Using scraps of yarn, make four twisted cords 11 inches (28 cm) long. Glue two of these to the inside of the back cover 6 inches (15.25 cm) from top and bottom, and two to the inside of the front cover, 5 inches (12.7 cm) from top and bottom. Glue the red felt to the inside of both covers.

With the hole punch make two holes at the left side edge of the paper. Place these inside the back of the folder and mark the position of the two holes with a pencil. Glue the center of the length of ribbon to the inside back cover between and over the position of the punched holes, leaving the ends free (see diagram). Glue a piece of posterboard over the ribbon to secure it in place. Thread ribbons through the holes in the paper and tie in a bow.

The chart for the Ark Folder is shown on pages 62–3.

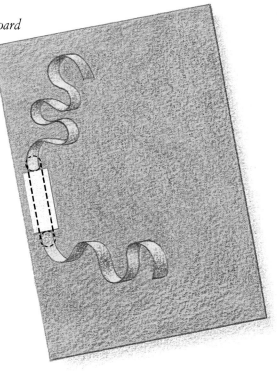

Inside back
Glue posterboard over ribbon to secure.

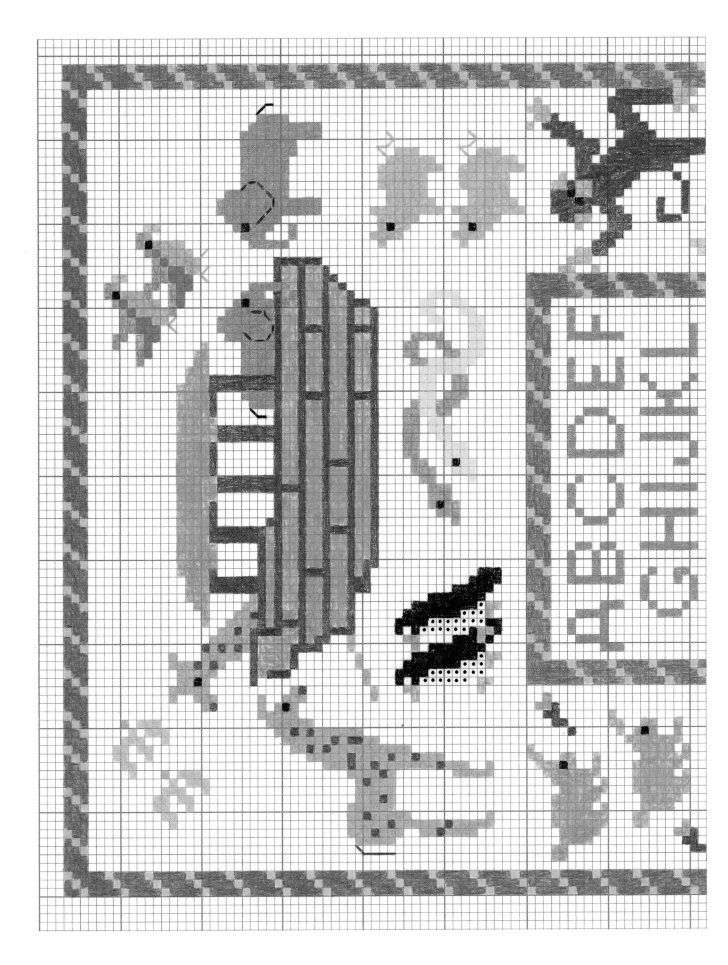

Ark Door Plate

This panel of cross-stitch can be used as a door plate, if protected with a suitable piece of Plexiglas®, or you could add a fringe and use it as a bookmark. Why not leave out the lovebirds and embroider your child's name instead, or choose your favorite animals to fill the panels?

Actual design measures: 2⅓ × 9½ in (5.9 × 24 cm)

Materials

1 piece of 14-count Aida measuring 3 × 11½ in (7.5 × 29.2 cm)
1 Plexiglas® door plate (see suppliers information on page 165)
No. 8 crewel needle
Cardboard
Glue

DMC 6-strand embroidery floss:

1 skein of gray (45)
1 skein of yellow (444)
1 skein of blue (798)
1 skein of aqua (518)
1 skein of pale green (954)
1 skein of brown (632)
1 skein of pale peach (3779)
1 skein of turquoise (995)
1 skein of black (310)
1 skein of red (606)
1 skein of green (906)

Instructions

Mark the center of the chart and the center of the Aida and, using three strands of floss, work in cross-stitch from here. Add details in straight stitch as indicated on the chart. When the embroidery is complete, mount it on a piece of cardboard the same size as the door plate by folding the excess fabric to the back and gluing it down or following the manufacturer's instructions.

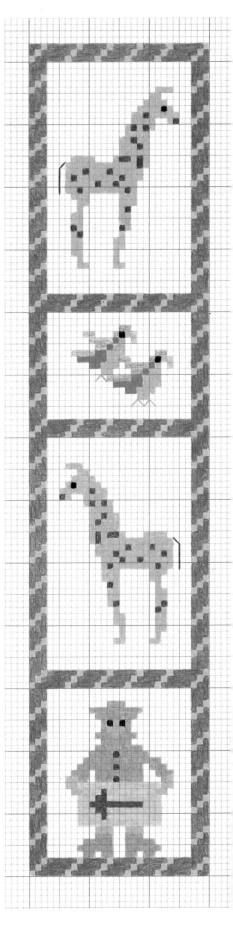

Ark Pencil Case

This handy pencil holder can be kept hanging on the wall or can be folded and used as a pencil case. I have used the same ticking for all these projects, but you could of course use a coordinating solid colored fabric if you preferred.

Actual design measures:
4½ × 11½ in (11.5 × 29.2 cm)

Materials

1 piece of 14-count Aida measuring 6½ × 13½ in (16.5 × 34.3 cm)
1 piece of cotton ticking or medium-weight fabric measuring 14 × 22 in (35.5 × 55.8 cm)
Sewing thread to match fabric
No. 8 crewel needle
Two small squares of self-adhesive Velcro®

DMC 6-strand embroidery floss:

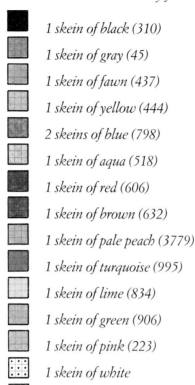

1 skein of black (310)
1 skein of gray (45)
1 skein of fawn (437)
1 skein of yellow (444)
2 skeins of blue (798)
1 skein of aqua (518)
1 skein of red (606)
1 skein of brown (632)
1 skein of pale peach (3779)
1 skein of turquoise (995)
1 skein of lime (834)
1 skein of green (906)
1 skein of pink (223)
1 skein of white
1 skein of greenish blue (954)

Instructions

Mark the center of the chart and the center of the Aida. Using three strands of floss, work from here in cross-stitch, adding detail in straight stitch as indicated on the chart. When the embroidery is complete, set it aside.

Turn under ½ inch (12 mm) on all sides of the ticking and hem in place. Fold up the bottom edge to make the pocket, approximately 6½ inches (16.5 cm) deep, and stitch the side seams. Pin the embroidery to the center of the pocket, folding back the excess Aida; leave a border of approximately ½ inch (12 mm) all around the finished embroidery. Stitch the side and bottom edges of this panel to the ticking.

Sew the Aida panel to the ticking pocket to form three separate channels for pencils, pens, etc. Make a 2-inch (5-cm) casing at the top of the ticking to hold a ruler. Affix two pieces of Velcro® at the back of the pencil holder with corresponding pieces stuck to the chosen position on the wall.

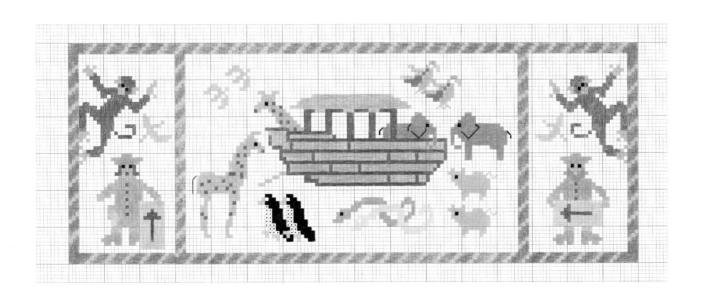

Ark Window Shade

It is easy to make a fabric window shade or stitch a border onto an existing one. Alternatively, you could use this design as a border along the edge of a shelf or on a valance over a curtain.

Actual design measures:
2½ × 21 in (6.3 × 53.3 cm)

Materials

*1 piece of 11-count Aida measuring
    5¾ in (14.6 cm) × the width
    of your window – minimum
    26 in (66 cm)*
*1 piece of cotton ticking or
    heavyweight cotton measuring the
    width of your window (with the
    same minimum as above) × the
    length plus 5 in (12.7 cm)*
No. 8 crewel needle
Shade roller to fit your window
*Wooden batten slightly narrower
    than the shade is wide*
*Small length of cord in a
    coordinating color*
1 bead

DMC 6-strand embroidery floss:

1 skein of black (310)
1 skein of gray (45)
1 skein of fawn (437)
1 skein of yellow (444)
1 skein of aqua (518)
1 skein of red (606)
1 skein of brown (632)
1 skein of pale peach (3779)
1 skein of turquoise (995)
1 skein of lime (834)
1 skein of green (906)
1 skein of pink (223)
1 skein of white
1 skein of greenish-blue (954)

Instructions

Mark the center of the chart and the center of the Aida. Start here, using four strands of floss to work the design in cross-stitch. Add straight stitch detail as indicated on the chart. When the embroidery is complete, set it aside.

Turn under and hem the long edges of your ticking to the required width. Turn under and stitch the top of the ticking, making a hem approximately 1 inch (2.5 cm) wide. Hem the bottom of the ticking about 2 inches (5 cm) from the bottom to form a casing. Stitch the embroidery to the shade using backstitch, or machine stitch it. Thread a length of cord through the bottom center of the shade. Thread on the bead and tie a knot in the cord to hold the bead in place.

Staple the top of the shade to a roller shade, and insert the batten into the bottom casing.

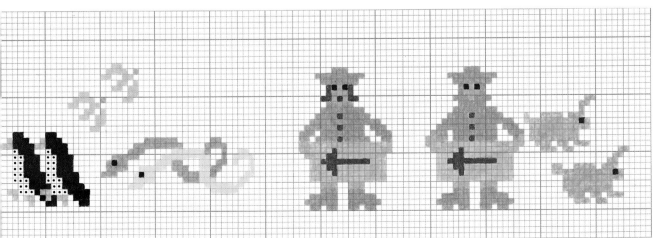

Bathrooms

SHELL
BATHROOM

Seashells, with their pretty pearly colors and interesting shapes, are a popular source of inspiration to both the embroiderer and the interior designer. Wallpapers, fabrics, borders, and stencils can be used in contrast or harmony to create a theme for a bathroom, and real shells displayed in flat baskets or glass bottles will add an extra decorative touch.

For the following projects, I have selected and emphasized the soft pinks and creams I associate with shells and drawn abstract shell shapes that will fit in with a modern interior. You might prefer a more delicate approach, in which case you could work these charts on a finer canvas or linen and use a palette of creams and golds for your embroidery. You might choose to follow a color scheme already dictated by a wallpaper or tile, but the important thing is to use your embroidery skills to accessorize your room with complementary images.

Shell Mirror Frame

I couldn't resist using a mirror image on this mirror frame design. You could add extra interest by incorporating some glittery thread or gluing real shells around the edge or on top of the design to make it three-dimensional. Pretty mirror frames have the advantage of improving the way you feel about yourself – especially first thing in the morning.

Actual design measures:
8¾ × 9 in (22.25 × 22.9 cm)

Materials
1 piece of 11-count Aida measuring
    12 in (30.5 cm) square
2 pieces of mat board, each
    measuring 8½ × 9¼ in (21.6 ×
    23.4 cm)
1 piece of polyester batting
    measuring 8½ × 9¼ in (21.6 ×
    23.4 cm)
1 sheet of paper measuring 9½ ×
    10 in (24 × 25.4 cm)
Pencil
Rubber-based adhesive
1¾ yards (1.5 meters) of colored
    cord for edging
1 piece mirror measuring a
    minimum of 4½ in (11.5 cm)
    square
No. 24 tapestry needle
Craft knife

DMC 6-strand embroidery floss:

2 skeins of rose (223)
2 skeins of pink (3779)
1 skein of silver (762)
1 skein of turquoise (518)
1 skein of light turquoise (519)
1 skein of gold (437)
1 skein of yellow (727)
1 skein of dark gray (451)
1 skein of white

Instructions
Mark the center of the Aida and the center of the chart and count outward from here to find a starting point for the design. Work the design entirely in cross-stitch using three strands of floss throughout.

Fold the paper in half vertically. Draw half an arched window shape against the center fold, using the template as a guide. Trace this shape onto both sheets of mat board and cut them out. Cut the center window in the same way from one piece of board only. Cut the batting to the same shape and glue into place on top of the piece of mat board with the cutout window.

Glue the finished embroidery to the board, stretching it over the cutout window, folding the excess over the edge and gluing it to the back of the board. With a craft knife, cut out the center of the Aida, leaving about ½ inch (12 mm) for folding to the back. Clip the margin perpendicularly to the window edge, turn back and glue to the mat board. Glue the mirror to the center of the other board, positioning it to correspond with the window opening. Glue the boards together. Carefully glue the cord around the edge of the mirror and the outer edge of the frame.

The chart for the Shell Mirror Frame is shown on pages 76–7, the template is below.

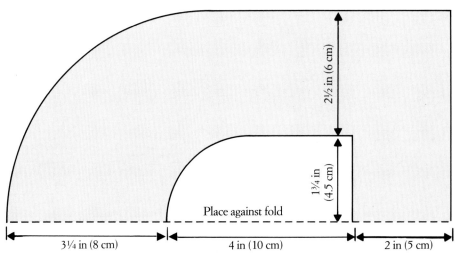

2½ in (6 cm)

1¾ in (4.5 cm)

Place against fold

3¼ in (8 cm)   4 in (10 cm)   2 in (5 cm)

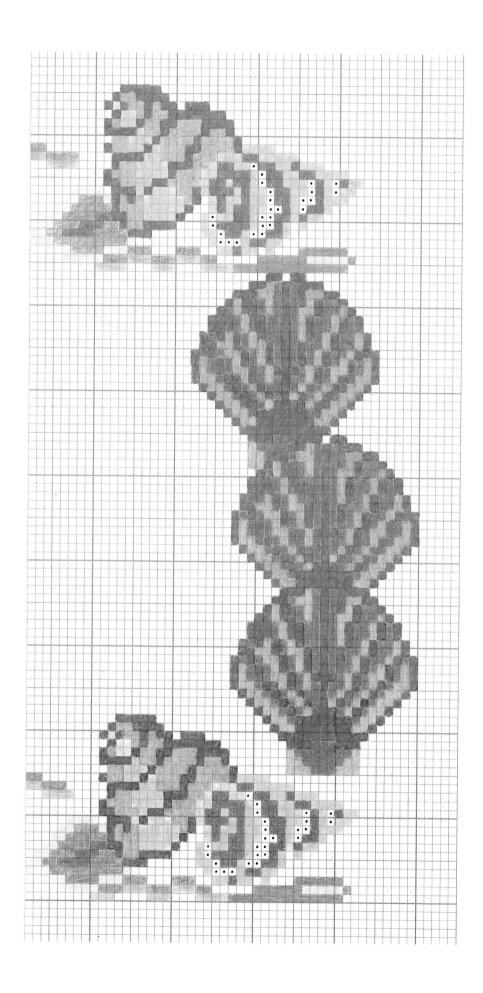

Shell Guest Towel

Many stores now sell towels with Aida borders ready for cross-stitching. If you have a plain towel that you want to use, simply cut a strip of Aida measuring approximately ½ inch (12 mm) more than your required width and depth, work your design on it and then fold the excess under and hand sew or machine stitch it in position on your towel. If you do not want to create a border design, you can stitch individual motifs over squares of waste canvas basted to the towel. Use an initial to personalize a very special gift.

Actual design measures:
2¾ × 6¾ in (7 × 17.1 cm)

Materials
1 guest towel with a strip of 14-count
Aida, or a strip of Aida to fit it
No. 24 tapestry needle

DMC 6-strand embroidery floss:

1 skein of steel gray (451)

1 skein of gray (453)

1 skein of tan (841)

1 skein of white

1 skein of gold (437)

1 skein of light turquoise (519)

1 skein of turquoise (518)

1 skein of pink (3779)

1 skein of rose (223)

1 skein of silver (762)

Instructions
Mark the center of the chart and the center of the Aida. Start here, working the design entirely in cross-stitch using three strands of floss.

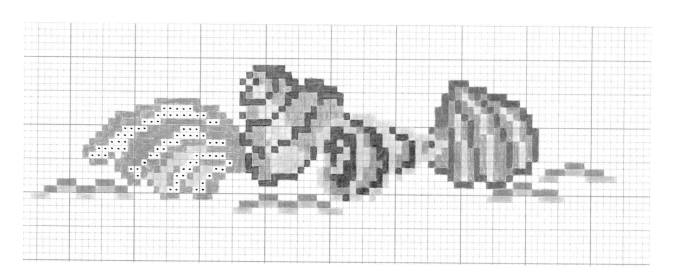

Shell Make-up Bag

This make-up or bathroom accessory bag can either be hung on the wall or folded up and taken on your travels. I have used a standard-sized guest towel and embroidered a Herta panel in soft cottons (floss). The real shells are added at the end to complete the picture.

Materials

Peach hand towel measuring
*   18 × 33 in (45.7 × 83.8 cm)*
1 piece of 6-count blue Herta
*   measuring 12 × 15 in*
*   (30.5 × 38 cm)*
1 spool of Kreinik gold cord
Sewing thread
No. 23 tapestry needle
10 small shells
Glue
Crochet hook

DMC Matte Coton:

1 skein of gray (451)
1 skein of butter (746)
1 skein of donkey (841)
1 skein of aqua (518)
1 skein of slate (414)
1 skein of rose (223)
1 skein of pink (225)
1 skein of silver (762)

Instructions

Mark the center of the chart and the center of the Herta. Start here, working the design in cross-stitch using a single thread of all colors except pink, which should be used together with one strand of gold cord. Work the main body of the design in cross-stitch and use star stitch (see the diagrams below) as indicated on the chart. When the design is finished, cut 6 × 10-inch (15.25 cm) lengths of embroidery cotton and lay them along the inside openings of the shells, leaving equal tails of thread loose at each end. Squeeze a line of glue on the top of each shell opening, over the embroidery cotton, and set aside to dry. When they are dry, thread the two ends into the holes nearest to the eight positions indicated on the chart. Tie securely at the back and cut off the excess.

Finishing

Fold under ½ inch (12 mm) on the edges of the completed embroidery. Position the embroidery at the center of the bottom edge of the towel and hand sew or machine stitch it in place. Put the towel in front of you, wrong side up, and fold the unembellished end to form a 12-inch (30.5 cm) deep pocket. Sew the side seams and make two further seams 6 inches (15.25 cm) apart to form three channels in which to keep your bathroom accessories. Pass the thread ends of the two remaining shells through the towel, positioning them approximately 1 inch (2.5 cm) from the bottom of the two center seams to act as buttons. With the crochet hook and two lengths of embroidery thread (see page 164), make two chains approximately 2 inches (5 cm) long and use to form two loops at the other end of the towel to correspond with the shell buttons. Make two more chains of embroidery thread and attach them at the sides of the towel, even with the top of your embroidered panel. These can be used to hang your bag from a dowel, or on a hook in your bathroom.

Star stitch is worked on a block of nine holes, working into each hole and back to the center each time.

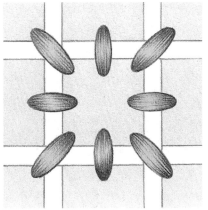

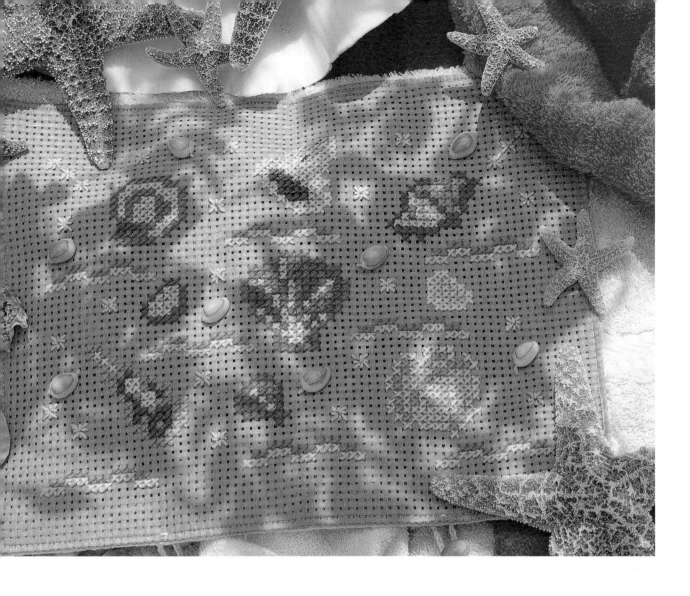

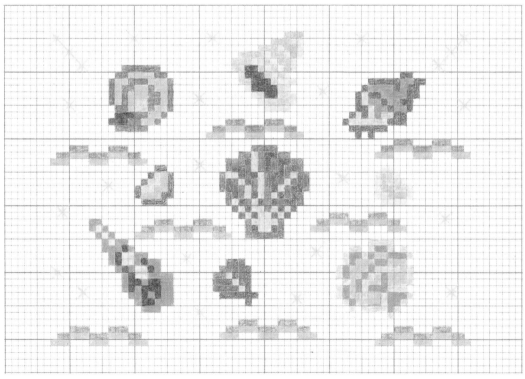

Shell Picture Frame

If you do not want to go the whole hog and embroider the stripes on this frame, you could work the motifs on perforated paper, cover a frame with striped fabric, and glue your embroidery on the corner. For added interest, you could glue some real shells along the outside of the frame and incorporate one or two real cockle shells into the embroidered design.

Actual design measures:
9 × 10 in (22.9 × 25.4 cm)

Materials
*1 piece of 14-count Aida measuring
 11 × 12 in (28 × 30.5 cm)
2 pieces of mat board, each
 measuring 9 × 10 in (22.9 × 25.4
 cm)
No. 8 crewel needle
Rubber-based adhesive
Craft knife
Pencil*

DMC 6-strand embroidery floss:

1 skein of dark gray (451)

1 skein of gray (762)

1 skein of yellow (727)

1 skein of gold (437)

3 skein of pale yellow (3078)

3 skeins of turquoise (518)

1 skein of pink (3779)

1 skein of rose (223)

1 skein of white

Instructions
Count 14 threads in on the left side and 14 threads up from the bottom of the Aida and begin here. Work the entire design in cross-stitch using two strands of floss. When the embroidery is complete, cut out the plain center panel to within ½ inch (12 mm) of the embroidery. Clip the corners carefully and fold the excess under, leaving a clean edge. Place the finished work on top of one piece of mat board and draw around the inner square with a pencil. Cut this shape from the mat board with a craft knife. Fold the edges of the Aida over the board, gluing them securely. Be sure the stripes remain straight. Lay the completed picture frame on top of the remaining piece of mat board and glue together along the sides and bottom, leaving the top open to slide in your photograph.

The chart for the Shell Picture Frame is shown on pages 84–5.

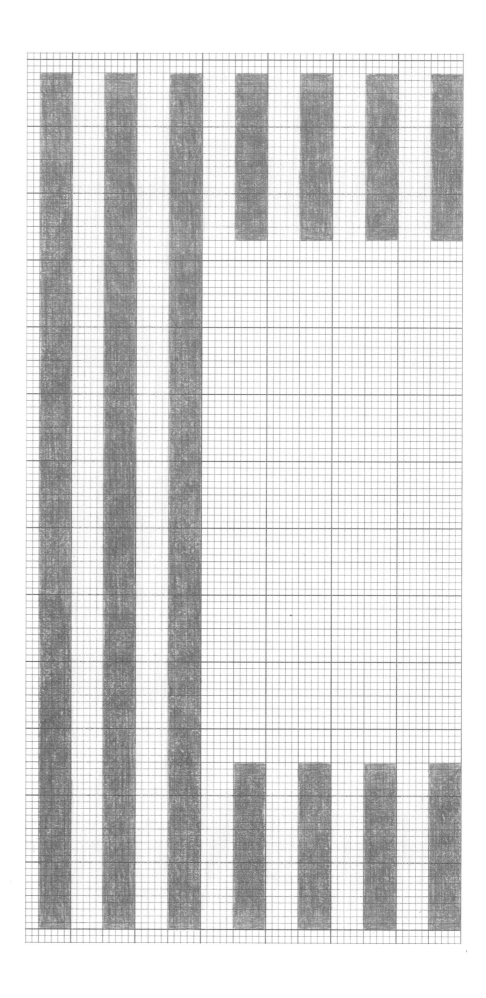

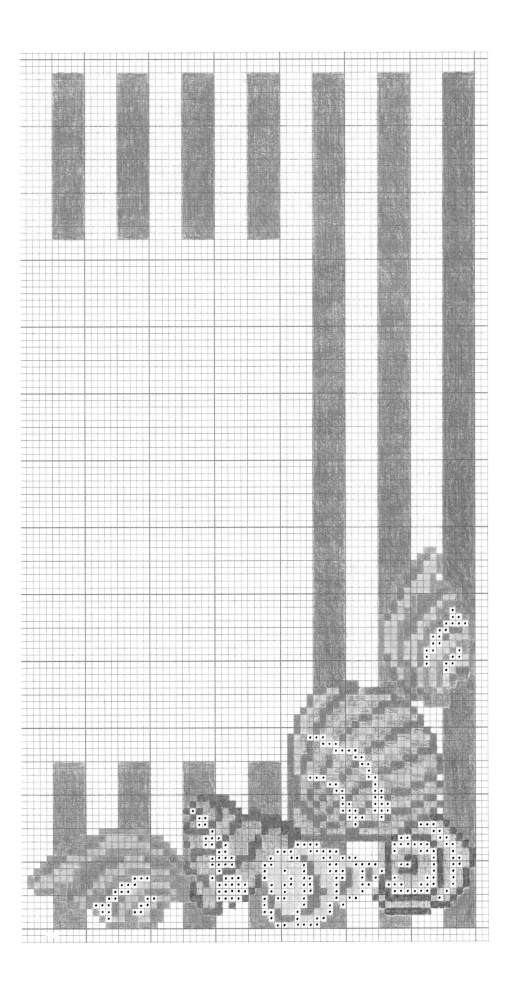

PENNSYLVANIA GERMAN BATHROOM

We have many reasons to thank the eighteenth and nineteenth-century homemakers of the rural mid-Atlantic region. Not only have they taught us a style of decoration that is timeless and practical, but the methods they used to achieve it have inspired craftspeople working in a vast array of mediums ever since.

From homespun patchworks to hand-painted furniture, the bold colors and stylized motifs typical of these communities have brightened our homes, and the simplicity of approach has shown that the desired end is not beyond our means.

Interpretations of boldly colored birds and flowers and the traditional symbols of folk art are strangely universal. Many similar motifs can be found in the handcrafts of Eastern Europe, Asia, and even Australasia, but it is perhaps the settlers of Pennsylvania who interpreted these motifs in a way that suggested the comfort and style that we still attempt to reproduce.

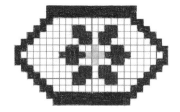

Folk Art Sampler

This project is a demonstration of how the stitching of motifs and borders can be practiced and at the same time arranged in a simple composition that warrants a frame in its own right. If you stitch because your creative instincts tell you to, put them into full flight and stitch simple motifs in your own choice of colors. Start with one image, maybe a bird or a flower, and work it in different positions, re-coloring and reversing it. Add a brightly colored border and an alphabet of your choice, and before you know it you will have created a central theme for your room and a piece of embroidery that is truly stamped with your own identity. The following sampler is intended only as a guide for you to begin with.

Actual design measures:
11½ × 12 in (29.2 × 30.5 cm)

Materials
One piece of 14-count Aida
   measuring 15 × 18 in
   (38 × 45.75 cm)
No. 24 tapestry needle

DMC 6-strand embroidery floss:

   1 skein of yellow (725)

   1 skein of turquoise (995)

   1 skein of green (701)

   1 skein of red (891)

   1 skein of pink (3609)

   2 skeins of fuchsia (718)

   1 skein of blue (340)

Instructions
Mark the center of the chart and
the center of the canvas. Using
three strands of floss, work from
here in cross-stitch until the design
is complete. Frame (see the
techniques on page 161) according
to taste, but keep it simple!

Folk Art Cabinet

This little cabinet is ideal for collectors. In the bathroom you could use it to display shells, coral or pebbles, or perhaps a collection of pill boxes. The central panel is worked on linen. You can use this idea with any of the small wood pieces designed for the display of embroidery. Mount your embroidery on lightweight cardboard and glue it into position.

Actual panel measures:
3½ in (8.9 cm) square
Actual design measures:
3 in (7.5 cm) square

Materials

Framecraft miniature cabinet
(see suppliers information on
page 165)
1 piece of 32-count linen measuring
5 in (12.7 cm) square
Lightweight cardboard
Glue
No. 8 crewel needle

DMC 6-strand embroidery floss:

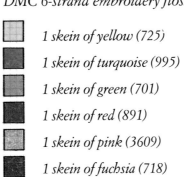

1 skein of yellow (725)

1 skein of turquoise (995)

1 skein of green (701)

1 skein of red (891)

1 skein of pink (3609)

1 skein of fuchsia (718)

Instructions

Mark the center of the chart and the center of the linen. Using two strands of floss over two threads of linen, work from here in cross-stitch throughout. When the embroidery is complete, mount on cardboard following the manufacturer's instructions and glue to the panel in the cabinet.

The chart for the American Folk Sampler is shown on pages 88–9.

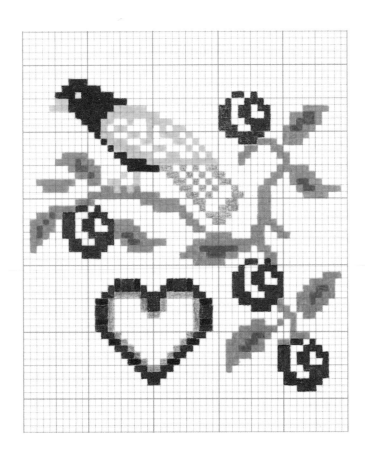

11¾ in (29.5 cm)

2¼ in (5.5 cm)

4½ in (11.5 cm)

Place against fold

Folk Curtain Tieback

This pattern can be used for lots of different projects. You could use it as a border across a window shade or as an edging for a shelf or series of shelves. You could also display it vertically as a bellpull. Add or omit as many of the motifs as you please according to the size you require.

Actual design measures:
2½ × 17 in (6.3 × 43 cm)

Materials
1 piece of 11-count Aida measuring
  5 × 20 in (12.7 × 51 cm)
2 pieces of backing material (I have
  used cotton chintz), each
  measuring 6 × 26 in (15.25 ×
  66 cm)
1 piece of buckram measuring 4 ×
  24 in (10 × 61 cm)
Tracing paper
Pencil
No. 24 tapestry needle
Small length of narrow ribbon for
  loops

DMC 6-strand embroidery floss:

1 skein of yellow (725)

1 skein of turquoise (995)

1 skein of red (891)

1 skein of pink (3609)

2 skeins of fuchsia (718)

Instructions
Leaving 1 inch (2.5 cm) of Aida at the left edge and top and bottom, begin working from the chart, in cross-stitch, using three strands of floss. Work the chart three times, then repeat the first block of eight stitches. Trace the template onto paper. Fold the buckram in half and lay the template on top with the straight edge against the fold; cut out. Cut two pieces of backing fabric, approximately ½ inch (12 mm) larger than the buckram all around. Sandwich the buckram in between, turn in and pin the excess edges of the backing, and machine stitch or hand sew together, inserting two loops of ribbon at the center of the short ends. Pin the embroidery along the center of the tieback, folding under the raw edges. Hand sew or machine stitch into position.

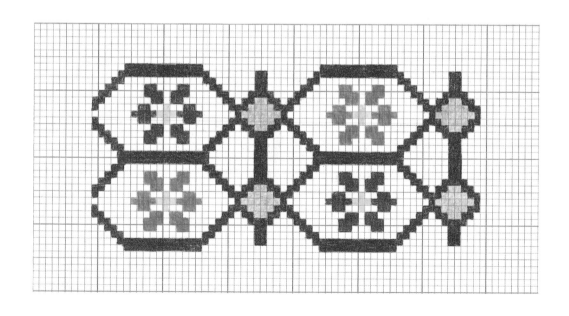

Folk Art Hook Panel

This panel could be mounted on a bathroom door for your bathrobe or it could be used to hold towels. The wooden panel with hooks was purchased, but you could make your own with a strip of 4½ × 12 inch (11.5 × 30.5 cm) wood and some ornamental hooks.

Actual design measures:
4½ × 12 in (11.5 × 30.5 cm)

Materials
*1 piece of 14-count Aida measuring
  15 × 18 in (38 × 45.7 cm)*
*1 piece of turquoise felt measuring
  11 × 16 in (28 × 40.6 cm)*
*1 piece of wood measuring 14 × 9 in
  (35.5 × 22.9 cm)*
*1 piece of wood measuring 5½ × 13
  in (14 × 33cm)*
*1 piece of polyester batting
  measuring 5½ × 15 in
  (14 × 33 cm)*
Rubber-based adhesive
No. 24 tapestry needle

DMC 6-strand embroidery floss:

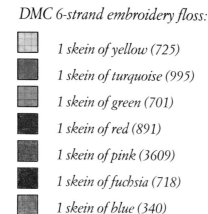

1 skein of yellow (725)

1 skein of turquoise (995)

1 skein of green (701)

1 skein of red (891)

1 skein of pink (3609)

1 skein of fuchsia (718)

1 skein of blue (340)

Instructions
Mark the center of the chart and the center of the Aida. Using three strands of floss, work from here in cross-stitch until the embroidery is complete. Glue the batting to the front of the smaller of the two pieces of wood. Stretch the embroidery over the padded board; wrap and glue the edges to the back. Glue the felt to the remaining board in the same way. Then glue the mounted embroidery to the felt-covered panel, centering it 1 inch (2.5 cm) down from the top.

If you are making your own panel, drill screw holes at each end for mounting and screw on your hooks at equally spaced intervals. Glue to the board underneath the mounted embroidery. Screw to a wall or door through the holes made in the hook panel, screwing through the felt-covered panel.

FRENCH TOILE
BATHROOM

The term "toile de Jouy" is given to a type of fabric first produced in 1770 at the Jouy factory in the village of Jouy-en-Josas near Versailles in France. The original designs were created using the copper-plate technique and printed onto Indian muslin; they often depicted pastoral scenes and pictorial images. The factory was extremely successful, and in 1806, the founder, German-born Christophe Philippe, set up a cotton mill in France with his brother.

The business advanced further by means of industrial espionage when the brothers visited England in 1810 to investigate various workshops and obtain information on machinery. This information was smuggled out of England through the use of invisible writing.

Natural dyes were used to color toile de Jouy, madder for the pinkish-reds, and indigo and woad for the blues, together with other vegetable dyes for the less popular hues. Many of the pictorial images that were featured were based on events of the time and therefore have historical significance.

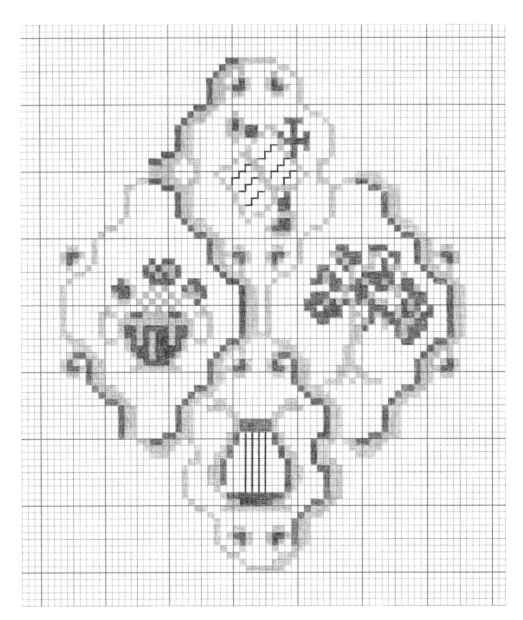

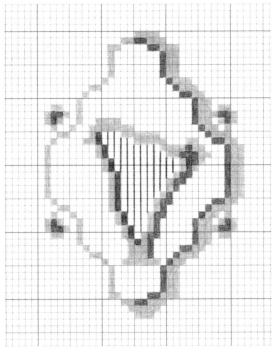

Toile de Jouy Brush and Mirror Set

This brush and mirror set is especially made for embroidery, but you may well find an old set at a flea market, yard sale, or auction. Silver-topped perfume bottles and crystal jars can also be purchased with blank panels for embroidery; they provide a rich and interesting collection for the boudoir.

If you have a plain-backed mirror or brush with an interesting border, you could mount your cross-stitch design on a piece of medium-weight cardboard and glue it to the back, but it is advisable to work your design on fine fabric to avoid bulkiness and creasing.

Actual design measures:
Mirror 4 × 5 in (10 × 12.7 cm);
Brush 2 × 2½ in (5 × 6.3 cm)

Materials
Framecraft silver brush and mirror set. This comes complete with a comb and can be bought at many good embroidery shops or by mail order (see the suppliers information on page 165)
For the mirror: one piece of 32-count Irish linen measuring 7 × 7½ in (17.8 × 19 cm)
For the brush: one piece of 32-count Irish linen measuring 5 × 6 in (12.7 × 15.25 cm)
No. 8 crewel needle
Cardboard

FOR THE MIRROR:
DMC 6-strand embroidery floss:

 1 skein of blue (827)

 1 skein of blue-gray (3752)

FOR THE BRUSH:
DMC 6-strand embroidery floss:

1 skein of blue (827)

1 skein of blue-gray (3752)

Instructions
Mark the center of the chart and the center of the linen. Starting here, work in cross-stitch and straight stitch as indicated on the charts. Use two strands of floss and stitch over two threads of linen. When the embroidery is complete, trim off the excess linen and mount on cardboard following the manufacturer's instructions.

Toile Candle Screen

This candle screen is especially made to show off embroidery and demonstrates the many unusual items that can be transformed with your cross-stitch skills. My stitchers particularly enjoyed making the projects in this section. Although they are produced on fine linen which requires a good light to work in, the fact that only two colors are used makes the stitching easier, and the end results are stunning. If you enjoy fine work, you might like to consider incorporating these design panels in a sampler or a firescreen. Of course, there is nothing to stop you from working on a coarser fabric and speeding up the process. For details of where to buy the candle screen, see the suppliers information on page 165.

Actual design measures:
2¾ × 3½ in (7 × 8.9 cm)

Materials
Framecraft candle screen (see
 suppliers information on
 page 165)
1 piece of 32-count linen measuring
 6 × 7 in (15.25 × 17.8 cm)
No. 8 crewel needle

DMC 6-strand embroidery floss:

 1 skein of moss green (3053)

 1 skein of dark moss green
(730)

Instructions
Mark the center of the chart and the center of the fabric and work from here in cross-stitch as indicated on the chart. Use two strands of floss and stitch over two threads of linen. When the embroidery is complete, mount according to the manufacturer's instructions.

Toile de Jouy Guest Towel

This evenweave hand towel in soft ivory is the perfect background for the soft subtle pinks used in this design. The towels can be purchased fringed (see the suppliers information on page 165), or you might like to use your own cotton guest towel and work the design over waste canvas. The towel I have used has 26 threads to the inch, and the embroidery should be worked over two threads. You can adjust the width by adding or subtracting lozenges or you might like to use this design as a border for a curtain or curtain tieback. You could also work the lozenges vertically as opposed to horizontally and create a bellpull.

Actual design measures:
4¾ × 12 in (12 × 30.5 cm)

Materials

1 evenweave guest towel measuring 15 in (38 cm) wide
No. 7 crewel needle

DMC 6-strand embroidery floss:

3 skeins of pink (224)
2 skeins of rose (223)

Instructions

Mark the center of the chart and, allowing a plain border of approximately 2 inches (5 cm), mark the middle of the towel. Work the design from here in cross-stitch and straight stitch as indicated on the chart. Use three strands of floss and stitch over two threads of fabric. You can create your own towel using Zweigart Linda fabric which is available in numerous colors. To create a quality appearance, however, I would suggest that you serge the side edges.

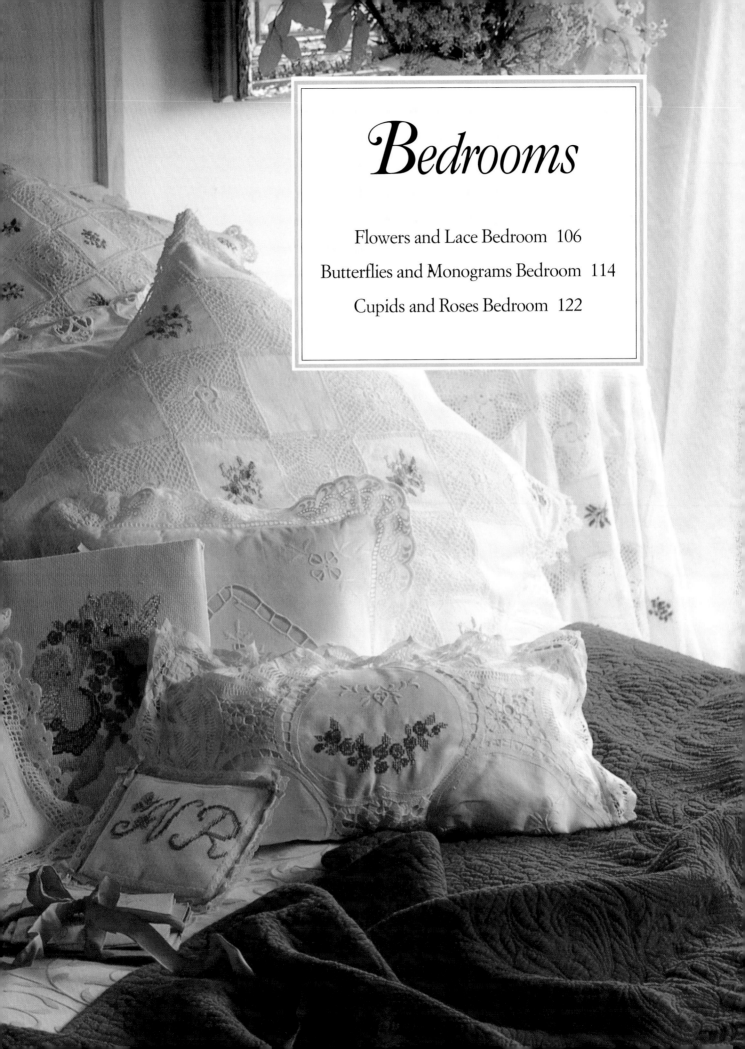

Bedrooms

FLOWERS AND LACE BEDROOM

Use these pretty wildflower motifs to decorate a lace bedroom. The pillow covers and bedspread lend themselves perfectly to embroidery as the panels allow you to work as many or as few flowers as you wish (see suppliers information on page 165). You can often pick up lace-trimmed items at auctions, or at church bazaars and yard sales. Why not embroider a single wildflower on the corner of a pillowcase or dot several over the hem on a sheet?

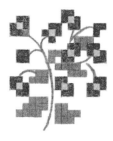

Lace Bedspread

This pretty spread is perfect for a summery bedroom. You can embroider as many panels as you wish.

Actual designs measure: approximately 1½ in (3.8 cm) square

Materials

Lace paneled bedspread measuring 72 × 90 in (183 × 229 cm)
42 pieces of 15-count waste canvas, each measuring 2½ in (6.3 cm) squarer
Contrasting sewing thread for basting
No. 8 crewel needle
Pair of tweezers

DMC 6-strand embroidery floss:

- *1 skein of green (905)*
- *1 skein of violet (552)*
- *1 skein of gold (743)*
- *1 skein of light blue (341)*
- *1 skein of yellow (725)*
- *1 skein of red (891)*
- *1 skein of lilac (3609)*
- *1 skein of pink (223)*
- *1 skein of medium blue (340)*
- *1 skein of coral (351)*
- *1 skein of dark blue (798)*

Instructions

Working across the width of the bedspread, center and baste the squares of waste canvas to the woven panels of the bedspread, working from right to left and positioning them as follows (or as desired):

Row 1: the first panel, then every fourth panel.
Row 2: the third panel, then every fourth panel.

Continue in sequence until every row has waste canvas stitched into place.

Mark the center of each motif and each square of canvas, and start stitching here. Using two strands of floss, work the motif from the chart in cross-stitch, stitching over two threads of canvas. Work the motifs in the order shown on the chart or in any sequence you wish. (Add straight stitch detail as indicated on the charts after waste canvas has been removed.) When the embroidery is finished, carefully remove the waste canvas from under the stitching with tweezers.

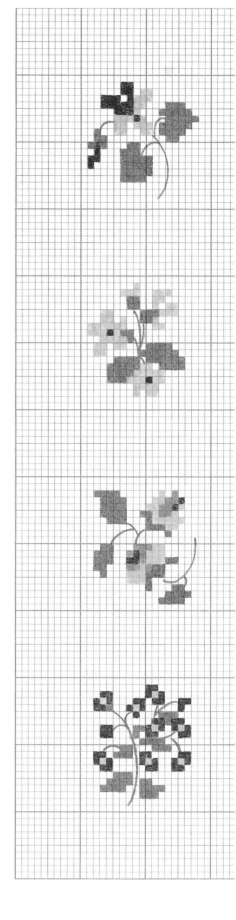

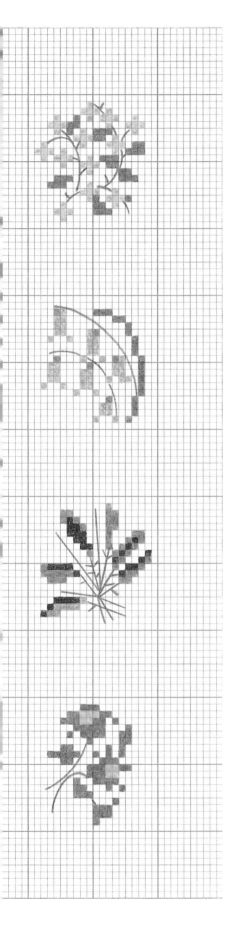

Wildflower Pillow

This pillow uses the same motifs as the Lace Bedspread, so is the ideal companion for it.

Actual designs measure: approximately 1½ in (3.8 cm) square

Materials

1 lace and cotton paneled pillow measuring 16 in (40.6 cm) square (see suppliers information on page 165)
16 pieces of 15-count waste canvas, each measuring 2½ in (6.3 cm) square
No. 8 crewel needle
Pair of tweezers

DMC 6-strand embroidery floss:

1 skein of green (905)
1 skein of violet (552)
1 skein of gold (743)
1 skein of light blue (341)
1 skein of yellow (725)
1 skein of red (891)
1 skein of lilac (3609)
1 skein of pink (223)
1 skein of medium blue (340)
1 skein of coral (351)
1 skein of dark blue (798)

Instructions

Baste the waste canvas to the center of each woven panel on the pillow cover. Mark the center of each chart and of each square of waste canvas. Starting here, work the eight charts over eight squares and then repeat for the second set of eight squares. Work in cross-stitch using two strands of floss over two threads of canvas. (Add stems in straight stitch, using two strands of floss, as indicated on the charts after waste canvas has been removed.) When the embroidery is complete, carefully remove the waste canvas from underneath the stitching with tweezers.

Rose and Forget-Me-Not Pillow

This design is worked on a larger version of the paneled pillow and features small posies of roses and forget-me-nots. I have chosen to place the design on every other panel, but you can, of course, work on each one if preferred. Alternatively, you could repeat one of the motifs from the Wildflower. Pillow – choose one that suits your decor.

Actual design measures:
2 × 2¼ in (5 × 5.7 cm)

Materials

1 lace and cotton paneled cushion, measuring 22 in (55.8 cm) square (see suppliers information on page 165)
8 pieces of 15-count waste canvas, each measuring 3 in (7.5 cm) square
No. 8 crewel needle
Pair of tweezers

DMC 6-strand embroidery floss:

1 skein of green (907)
1 skein of medium blue (340)
1 skein of yellow (725)
1 skein of peach (224)
1 skein of coral (351)
1 skein of rose (223)
1 skein of red (817)

Instructions

Baste the waste canvas to the center of every other woven panel on the pillow cover. Mark the center of each chart and of each square of waste canvas. Starting here, work the motif from the chart using two strands of floss, working in cross-stitch over two threads of canvas. (Add stems in straight stitch using two strands of floss after the waste canvas has been removed.) When the embroidery is complete, carefully remove the waste canvas from under the embroidery using tweezers.

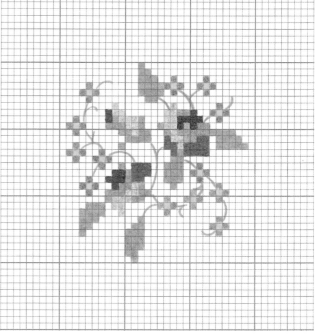

Spring Bouquet Heart

This little heart is designed for use as a potpourri sachet. The hearts can be bought in two separate halves, ready for embroidery (see suppliers information on page 165), or you could make your own from white cotton or linen fabric and lace trim. The spring bouquet could be used together with an initial (see pages 116–7) to decorate the corner of a pillowcase, or repeated continuously as a border for a photo frame. If you choose this last option, edge the design with two or three rows of plain cross-stitch in blue or pink.

Actual design measures:
2 × 2¼ in (5 × 5.7 cm)

Materials
Either a purchased cotton and lace heart (see suppliers information on page 165) or 2 pieces of white cotton or linen, each measuring 6 in (15.25 cm) square and 1 yard (90 cm) of 1-in (2.5-cm) wide lace trimming
1 piece of 15-count waste canvas, measuring 3 in (7.5 cm) square
Tracing paper
White sewing thread
No. 8 crewel needle
Pair of tweezers
Potpourri

DMC 6-strand embroidery floss:

1 skein of green (906)
1 skein of blue (800)
1 skein of yellow (743)
1 skein of peach (754)
1 skein of light pink (894)
1 skein of blue (798)
1 skein of orange (3340)
1 skein of white
1 skein of cherry (326)
1 skein of pink (892)

Instructions
If you are making the heart yourself, trace and complete the half-heart pattern below. Cut it out and pin it to the fabric and cut out two pieces. Using two strands of white floss, work buttonhole stitch around the edges of both heart shapes to keep them from fraying. Set one heart aside and baste the waste canvas to the center of the other. Work the design from the the chart in cross-stitch, using two strands of floss and working over two threads of canvas. (Using two strands of floss, work the detail in straight stitch as indicated on the chart after waste canvas has been removed.) When the embroidery is complete, carefully remove the waste canvas from underneath the stitching with tweezers.

Finishing
Leave two 2-inch (5-cm) ends of lace at center top, pin, then baste the lace all around the wrong side of embroidered heart, positioning it as shown in the photograph, and beginning and ending at the notch of the heart so that the ends of the lace form a hanging loop. Place the second heart under the first and stitch together, sandwiching the lace between, leaving a small opening on one side. Insert the potpourri, then close the opening.

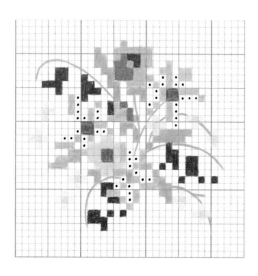

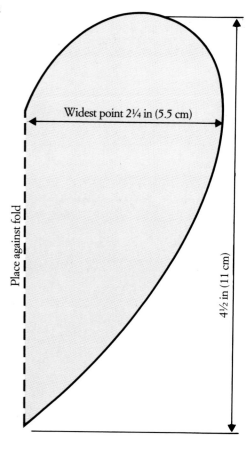

Widest point 2¼ in (5.5 cm)

Place against fold

4½ in (11 cm)

Little Rose Heart

This is worked in exactly the same way as the Spring Bouquet Heart, except that I have used a motif from the Lace Bedspread/ Wildflower Pillow. It would be particularly appropriate to fill this heart with dried rose petals. If you don't want to use a special potpourri, take a small piece of batting and sprinkle on a few drops of your favorite essential oil. Place this inside the heart instead of the flower petals.

Actual design measures:
1½ in (3.8 cm) square

Materials

*1 cotton and lace heart (see Spring
    Bouquet Heart)*
*1 piece of 15-count waste canvas,
    measuring 2 in (5 cm) square*
No. 8 crewel needle
Sewing thread for basting

DMC 6-strand embroidery floss:

▢	*1 skein of green (905)*
▤	*1 skein of coral (351)*
▦	*1 skein of pink (223)*
▪	*1 skein of red (891)*

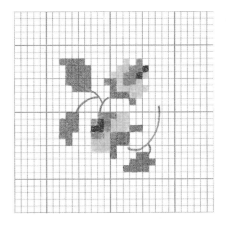

Instructions
Follow the instructions for the Spring Bouquet Heart opposite.

BUTTERFLIES AND MONOGRAMS BEDROOM

Given the time it takes to complete a piece of embroidery, a signature really is in order, and numerous books on alphabets are available to enable you to create your very own trademark. You might take the initial of your name and place it next to your favorite motif, or work the motif into your initial to create a complete picture. Traditional samplers have almost always featured an alphabet supplemented by messages, mottos, and proverbs embroidered in the same style.

As a result, traditional samplers look charming in traditional decors and the letters on the following chart can be used as shown to make a sampler, or worked as individual motifs. I have based my alphabet on a classic script but you should not feel limited by my choice of lettering style or my butterfly motifs since, with some tracing and graph paper and a little imagination, you can personalize any item in *your* signature style.

Butterfly Sampler

For this project I charted an alphabet and, as an afterthought, decided to create a butterfly border with a melange of colors and positions. Given the nature of the creatures, it was inevitable that one or two would fly into the main body of the design and make their presence known.

Actual design measures:
12 × 15½ in (30.5 × 39.5 cm)

Materials
1 piece of 18-count Aida measuring
15 × 18 in (38 × 45.75 cm)
No. 8 crewel needle

DMC 6-strand embroidery floss:

- *2 skeins of blue (333)*
- *2 skeins of light blue (340)*
- *1 skein of coral (351)*
- *1 skein of pink (776)*
- *1 skein of yellow (727)*
- *1 skein of gold (725)*
- *1 skein of green (907)*
- *1 skein of mauve (552)*
- *1 skein of lilac (553)*
- *1 skein of red (606)*
- *1 skein of yellow (727)*
- *1 skein of brown (632)*

Instructions
Mark the center of the chart (see pages 116–7) and the center of the fabric. Work from here in cross-stitch using two strands of floss and working over two threads of linen. Work butterfly antennae in straight stitch. Frame as you wish (see page 161).

Nightgown Case with Monogram

One of my favorite occupations is to hunt through bundles of household fabrics at yard sales and auctions in the hope that a beautiful piece of handmade lace work will surface. So I find it rather unsporting — but surely convenient — that department stores stock handmade, lace-trimmed linens that look exactly like rare antiques but are in fact just a few weeks old. My nightgown case with its lace edging and insets is in fact one of those new pieces and I think it has been enhanced by the hand embroidery.

If you have an old lace-trimmed dresser scarf or table runner, you could easily make a similar case. Simply fold it in thirds, stitch two layers together at the edges, and fold the top third over for a flap. Then add an initial and a motif. Scraps of lace and cotton can be salvaged to make all kinds of pretty bedroom accessories, from tissue cases to box tops. Do not discard old fabrics because they are torn or stained, just cut away the offending area and think creatively about what is left.

Actual design measures:
2½ × 3in (6.3 × 7.5 cm)

Materials
Old lace pochette or lace-trimmed
square plus a strip of cotton or
linen fabric twice its length
1 piece of 15-count waste canvas
measuring 4 in (10 cm) square
White sewing thread
No. 8 crewel needle
Pair of tweezers

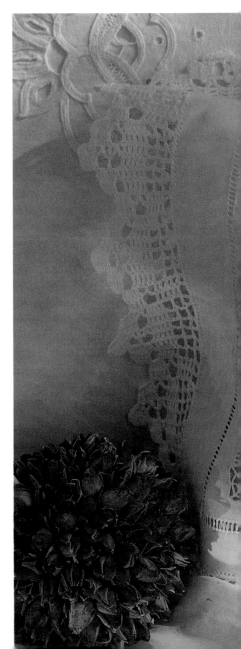

DMC 6-strand embroidery floss:

- 1 skein of pink (776)
- 1 skein of coral (351)
- 1 skein of green (907)
- 1 skein of lilac (553)
- 1 skein of green (451)
- 1 skein of blue (333)
- 1 skein of light blue (340)
- 1 skein of yellow (727)

Instructions

Baste the waste canvas to the center of the lace-trimmed square or the flap of the pockette. Select and rechart your initial with a butterfly positioned to hover over the flowers, as shown in the photograph. Mark the center of the chart and the center of the waste canvas and work in cross-stitch from here, using two strands of floss over two threads of canvas. (Add the butterfly's antennae using straight stitches after the waste canvas has been removed.) When the embroidery is complete, carefully remove the waste canvas

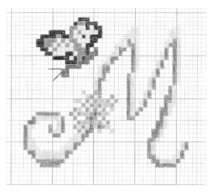

from underneath the stitching.

If you are making your own case, fold your strip of cotton in half and sew up the side seams. Stitch the embroidered square to the top back edge to form a flap.

Monogram Sachet

Small sachets make lovely gifts and can be used to decorate and scent a bedroom. They also provide you with a good use for scraps of embroidery fabric and floss. Back them with bits of curtain fabric for a coordinated look and trim with ribbon and lace.

Actual design measures:
2½ × 4½ in (6.3 × 11.5 cm)

Materials

1 piece of 30-count linen measuring 3½ × 5½ in (8.9 × 14 cm)
1 piece of backing fabric measuring 3½ × 5½ in (8.9 × 14 cm)
1 piece of batting measuring 5 × 10 in (12.7 × 25.4), perfumed with a few drops of essential oil
1 piece of lace ¾ in (19 mm) wide × 29½ in (75 cm) long
1 piece of ribbon ¾ in (19 mm) wide × 29½ in (75 cm) long
4 ribbon bows
White sewing thread
No. 8 crewel needle

DMC 6-strand embroidery floss:

1 skein of gold (725)
1 skein of pink (224)
1 skein of coral (351)
1 skein of gray (451)
1 skein of green (907)
1 skein of turquoise (518)
1 skein of light turquoise (3761)
1 skein of yellow (727)

Instructions

Referring to the photograph, select and rechart your initials with a butterfly positioned to hover nearby. Do not use the flower motif on the second initial but continue the line of the letter instead. Mark the center of the chart and the center of the linen and work the design in cross-stitch using two strands of floss over two threads of linen. Complete the butterfly motif by adding the antennae in straight stitches.

When the embroidery is finished, pin it to your backing fabric, turning in approximately ¼ inch (6 mm) all around both the back and front edges. Stitch together along the bottom and sides, fold the perfumed batting in half and insert in the top, then sew along the top. Sew lace and ribbon around the outer edge and add a bow on each corner.

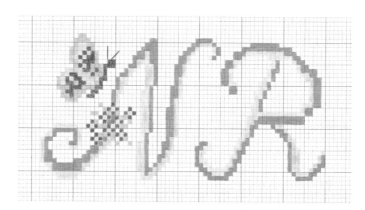

Pillowcase with Monogram

Add an initial to a pillowcase or the corner of the hem of a sheet. You could also decorate a plain white duvet with butterflies or make a sampler using just the butterfly motifs in different colors and frame it so it looks like a collection of the real things.

Actual design measures: approximately 3 in (7.5 cm) square depending on the initial chosen

Materials
Plain white pillowcase
1 piece of 15-count waste canvas measuring 4 in (10 cm) square
No. 8 crewel needle
Sewing thread for basting
Pair of tweezers

DMC 6-strand embroidery floss:

1 skein of coral (351)

1 skein of pink (776)

1 skein of yellow (727)

1 skein of light blue (340)

1 skein of blue (333)

1 skein of gray (451)

1 skein of green (907)

Instructions
Baste the waste canvas at an angle near the corner of the pillowcase. Select and rechart your initial with a butterfly positioned to hover over the flowers. Mark the center of the chart and the center of the waste canvas. Starting here, work in cross-stitch using two strands of floss over two threads of canvas. When the embroidery is complete, carefully remove the waste canvas from under the stitching with a pair of tweezers.

CUPIDS AND ROSES BEDROOM

Cupid or Amorino fits perfectly into a bedroom setting because he has been identified by the Greeks as Eros, god of love, and by the Romans as the son of Venus. It is not quite clear who his father was — some believe him to be Jupiter, others Mars or Mercury — but this chubby little cherub certainly played a very important role in the art and architecture of the Renaissance and Baroque periods, and he is currently enjoying a popular revival. Cupid's lead arrow is the symbol of sensual love, while his golden arrow symbolizes virtuous love. He is often depicted in art and sculpture carrying a bow and arrow or strewn with garlands of flowers like the winged celestial spirit featured in the following projects.

Swag of Roses

This small swag of roses is used here as a detail on a square Battenburg lace doily, which is folded in half to form an oblong pillow. It can also be repeated as a border for a pillowcase or worked as a mirror image for a photo frame. If worked on a lower-count fabric, you could use the swag as a curtain tieback — pretty for plain lace curtains.

Actual design measures:
2 × 5 in (5 × 12.7 cm)

Materials

1 square Battenburg lace doily measuring 16 in (40.6 cm) square
1 pillow form or roll of polyester batting 16 in (40.6 cm) long
1 piece of 15-count waste canvas measuring 4 × 6 in (10 × 15.25 cm)
White sewing thread
No. 8 crewel needle
Pair of tweezers

DMC 6-strand embroidery floss:

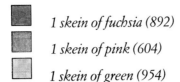

1 skein of fuchsia (892)
1 skein of pink (604)
1 skein of green (954)

Instructions

Baste the waste canvas into the required position on the lace doily. Mark the center of the chart and the center of the waste canvas.

Starting here, work the design in cross-stitch using two strands of floss over two threads of canvas. When the embroidery is complete, carefully remove the strands of waste canvas from underneath the stitching with the tweezers.

Fold the lace doily in half over the pillow form or roll of batting and sew at the side and bottom edges.

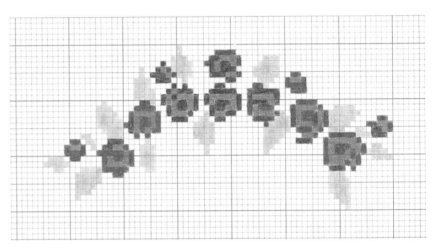

Cupid on Perforated Paper

There are numerous uses for embroidered motifs worked on perforated paper. They can be glued to screens to add special interest to a découpage project. They are effective hung from a tree as Christmas decorations, worked as bookmarks and greeting cards, backed and hung as mobiles, or used in this way as an isolated motif cut to shape and glued to a picture or mirror frame.

Actual design measures:
5 × 5½ in (12.7 × 14 cm)

Materials

1 piece of 14-count perforated paper, measuring 7 in (17.8 cm) square
1 spool of Kreinik Ombre Silver 1000
No. 7 crewel needle
Rubber-based adhesive
Small pair of sharp-pointed scissors

DMC 6-strand embroidery floss:

- 1 skein of yellow (743)
- 1 skein of gold (725)
- 1 skein of red (606)
- 1 skein of peach (224)
- 1 skein of pale peach (754)
- 1 skein of blue (798)
- 1 skein of light blue (809)
- 1 skein of fuchsia (892)
- 1 skein of pink (604)
- 1 skein of green (954)
- 1 reel of Kreinik Silver (see left)

Instructions

Mark the center of the chart (see bottom of page 128) and the center of the perforated paper. Starting here, work in cross-stitch using three strands of floss; use two strands of silver thread for the wings. When the embroidery is complete, cut away the excess paper around Cupid, taking care not to cut into a hole in which a stitch is worked. Finish off the ends at the back of the work and glue them down with a rubber-based adhesive. Glue to the mirror or photo frame of your choice.

Cupid Jewelry Holder

Here is a neat way to display your jewelry and decorate your dresser. The side panels are attached with tape to form mock hinges and, while I have covered them with satin, you could use lace, leftover chintz, or any fabric that takes your fancy. Stitch lengths of ribbon onto the side boards to tie on your jewelry, as shown in the photograph.

Actual design measures:
6 × 7½ in (15.25 × 19 cm)

Materials

1 piece of 14-count Aida measuring
  9½ × 12 in (24 × 30.5 cm)
2 pieces of satin fabric, each
  measuring 5½ × 12 in
  (14 × 30.5 cm)
2 pieces of polyester batting, each
  measuring 3½ × 10 in
  (8.9 × 25.4 cm)
1 piece of polyester batting
  measuring 7½ × 10 in
  (10 × 25.4 cm)
2 pieces of cardboard, each
  measuring 3½ × 10 in (8.9 ×
  25.4 cm)
1 piece of cardboard measuring
  7½ × 10 in (19 × 25.4 cm)
1 piece of felt measuring 10 × 13 in
  (25.4 × 33 cm)
Clean towel
Heavy-duty tape 2 in (5 cm) wide
  (carpet tape is ideal)
Rubber-based adhesive
1 spool of Kreinik Ombre Silver
  1000
No. 7 crewel needle
1¼ yards (1 meter) of ¼-in (8-mm)
  wide satin ribbon

DMC 6-strand embroidery floss:

1 skein of yellow (743)
1 skein of gold (725)
1 skein of red (606)
1 skein of peach (224)
2 skeins of pale peach (754)
1 skein of blue (798)
1 skein of light blue (809)
1 skein of fuchsia (892)
1 skein of pink (604)
1 skein of green (954)
1 reel of Kreinik Silver
(see left)

Instructions

Mark the center of the chart (made up of the two Cupids on page 128 joined together) and the center of the Aida. Starting here, work the design in cross-stitch using three strands of floss. Work the wings using two strands of silver thread. Glue a corresponding piece of polyester batting onto each piece of cardboard. Center the finished embroidery face up over the largest piece of padded cardboard; wrap and glue the excess to the back. Cover the two remaining pieces of padded cardboard with satin fabric in the same way. Place the three covered boards face down on a clean towel and line them up with the embroidered board in the center. Leaving enough slack in between to allow the side boards to fold back, join the boards with vertical strips of heavy-duty tape. Finally, glue the piece of felt over the three boards to hide the seams and raw edges.

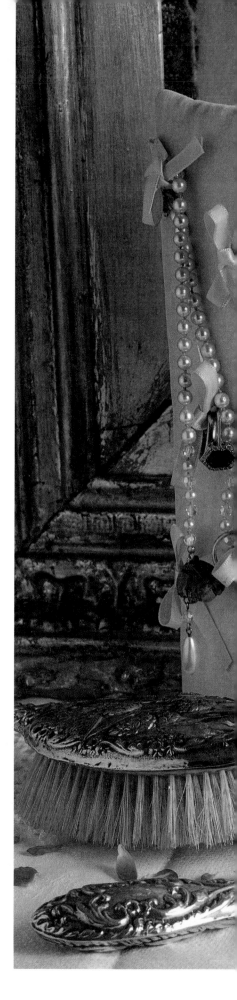

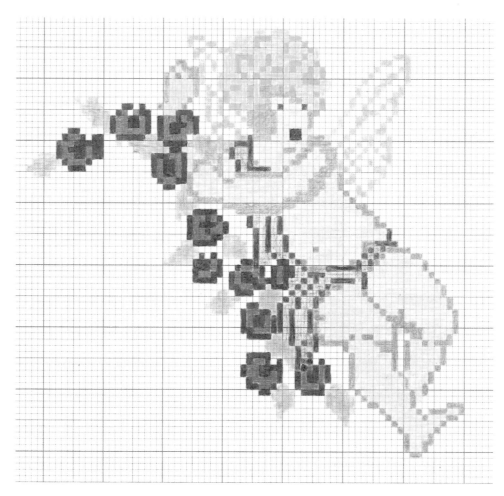

Cupid Runner

For this project I have worked Cupid horizontally to make him look as if he is flying (see the top chart on the facing page). This piece of embroidery is worked in the center of a placemat, which can be used on a dressing table. If you prefer, you can back the placemat with fabric to make a pillow or drape it over a chair back. If you use it as a pillow, scent it with a sachet of potpourri inserted with the padding.

Actual design measures:
4 × 6 in (10 × 15.25 cm)

Materials
1 lace and cotton placemat measuring 13 × 20 in (33 × 51 cm) — see suppliers information on page 165
1 piece of 15-count waste canvas measuring 5 × 7 in (12.7 × 17.8 cm)
1 spool of Kreinik Ombre Silver 1000
Sewing thread for basting
No. 8 crewel needle
Pair of tweezers

DMC 6-strand embroidery floss:

1 skein of yellow (743)

1 skein of gold (725)

1 skein of red (606)

1 skein of peach (224)

2 skeins of pale peach (754)

1 skein of blue (798)

1 skein of light blue (809)

1 skein of fuchsia (892)

1 skein of pink (604)

1 skein of green (954)

1 reel of Kreinik Silver (see left)

Instructions
Baste the waste canvas onto the center of the placemat. Mark the center of the chart (see the top of page 128) and the center of the waste canvas. Starting here, work in cross-stitch using two strands of floss or silver thread over two threads of canvas. When the embroidery is complete, carefully remove the strands of waste canvas from under the stitching with the tweezers.

Living Rooms

MIX-AND-MATCH
LIVING ROOM

This section is intended to encourage you to produce your own designs from the fabrics, wallpapers, and china in your home. I have used a Limoges dish and an antique Royal Cauldon side plate as inspiration and, having transformed sections of the designs into charts, I have used the motifs as decorations for table linens, a pillow cover, and a bellpull. Shortcuts to designing and creating your own charts are explained in the techniques section (see pages 158–164) and, having grasped the principles, you will find you can transform all your favorite motifs into cross-stitch designs that will happily mix and match.

Limoges Cloth

This linen doily, edged in Battenburg lace, was made in modern China. You could use it under a centerpiece on a dining table or as a cloth for an occasional table. Alternatively, you could back it with white linen and turn it into a pillow. The design is taken from the center of my dish, which also has a pretty painted gold frame that would not translate well into cross-stitch. Very crafty souls could add the gold detail with fabric paint or embroider it in satin stitch with gold thread.

Actual design measures:
2½ × 6¾ in (6.3 × 17.1 cm)

Materials
1 lace-edged linen doily measuring
   14 in (35.5 cm) square
4 pieces of 15-count waste canvas,
   each measuring 3 × 7½ in
   (7.5 × 19 cm)
Contrasting sewing thread for
   basting
No. 8 crewel needle
Pair of tweezers

DMC 6-strand embroidery floss:

1 skein of yellow (727)
1 skein of rust (900)
1 skein of green (699)
1 skein of light green (414)
1 skein of pink (3609)
1 skein of peach (754)
1 skein of rose (3687)
1 skein of blue (340)
1 skein of mauve (210)
1 skein of black (310)

Instructions

Position the waste canvas on the doily approximately 3 inches (7.5 cm) in from the edges. Baste the two strips in place using contrasting thread. Mark the center of the charts (noting that the design is reversed on alternate edges of the doily) and the center of the waste canvas and, starting here, work the design in cross-stitch using two strands of floss over two threads of canvas. When the embroidery is complete, carefully pull the strands of waste canvas from under the stitching with the tweezers.

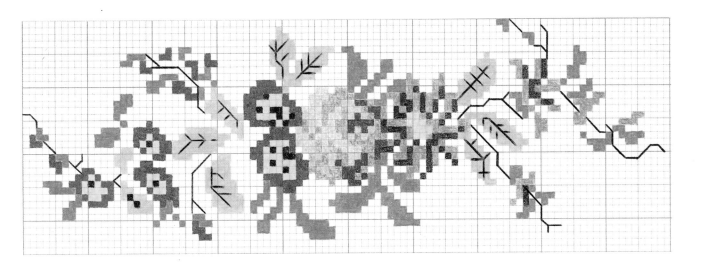

Mix-and-Match Bellpull

You could work a bellpull in either of my two designs or make your own. The long narrow shape of the fabric lends itself to repeat border designs and a wallpaper frieze could provide the perfect inspiration for this project. I have taken separate floral motifs from my tea plate and rearranged and reversed them to form a panel.

Actual design measures:
3½ × 14½ in (8.9 × 36.8 cm)

Materials
1 piece of 14-count Aida measuring
   5 × 18 in (12.7 × 45.7 cm)
1 piece of backing fabric 1½ in
   (3.8 cm) longer than the Aida
1¼ yards (1 meter) of satin cord
1 bell
Sewing thread to match backing
   fabric
No. 24 tapestry needle

DMC 6-strand embroidery floss:

1 skein of yellow (727)
1 skein of blue (340)
1 skein of light green (834)
1 skein of dark pink (602)
1 skein of purple (550)
1 skein of medium pink (604)
1 skein of gold (725)
1 skein of lavender (333)
1 skein of green (905)
1 skein of rust (900)
1 skein of light pink (963)
1 skein of light blue (809)

Instructions
Mark the center of the chart and the center of the Aida. Starting here, work the design in cross-stitch using three strands of embroidery floss. When the embroidery is complete, place it right side up on the wrong side of the backing fabric. Allow an extra 1 inch (2.5 cm) of backing fabric at the top and an extra ½ inch (12 mm) at the bottom. Fold in all side edges, letting backing extend slightly beyond Aida, and sew together. Turn the backing fabric and Aida under at the bottom edge, leaving a small casing of backing fabric showing at the front (see photograph). Stitch together. Fold in the Aida and the backing fabric at the top, making the edges flush. Stitch together, leaving openings at the side through which to pass the cord. Insert the cord and tie on the bell.

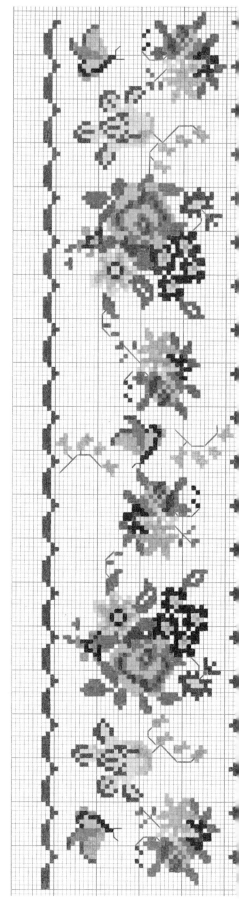

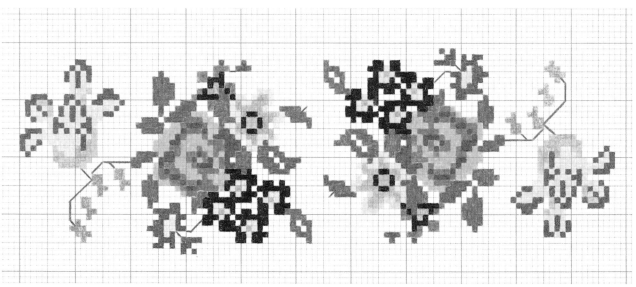

Mix-and-Match Bolster

I have used a purchased bolster for this design, but instructions are given for one that is very easy to make. Bolster forms are available from most good furnishing or department stores and you can make the cover from linen, sheeting, or a piece of antique lace. The following instructions are for a plain cover which you could decorate with ribbon ties at each end.

Actual design measures;
2¾ × 7½ in (7 × 19 cm)

Materials
1 piece of linen measuring 33 × 34 in (83.8 × 86.3 cm)
2 lengths of ¾-in (2-cm) wide ribbon approximately 27½ in (69.8 cm) long
1 piece of 15-count waste canvas measuring 4 × 9½ in (10 × 24 cm)
Sewing thread to match fabric
No. 8 crewel needle
Pair of tweezers
1 small bolster form

DMC 6-strand embroidery floss:

1 skein of yellow (727)
1 skein of blue (340)
1 skein of light green (834)
1 skein of dark pink (602)
1 skein of medium pink (604)
1 skein of gold (725)
1 skein of lavender (333)
1 skein of green (905)
1 skein of rust (900)
1 skein of light pink (963)
1 skein of light blue (809)

Instructions
Sew 1 inch (2.5 cm) casings on the two shorter edges of the fabric. Fold the fabric in half with the shorter edges meeting, crease lightly, unfold. Center and baste the waste canvas over the crease. Mark the center of the chart and the center of the canvas. Starting here, work the design in cross-stitch using two strands of floss over two threads of canvas. When the embroidery is complete, carefully remove the strands of canvas from under the stitching using tweezers. Fold the fabric in half, right sides together and long edges meeting, and join 1 inch (2.5 cm) from the raw edges. Turn right side out and thread the ribbon through the casing. Place the cover over the bolster form and gather both ends, securing with bows.

Mix-and-Match Tablecloth

Take a plain or patterned tablecloth and work small motifs randomly or group them to complement a lace design. If you are working on a plain cloth, edge it with a one-color, two-row border and create a panel in the center by stitching another border. Alternatively, select single flower heads and dot them on the cloth. Why not make some napkins to match as well?

Actual designs measure:
1½ in (3.8 cm) square and
4 in (10 cm square)

Materials
1 square tablecloth
4 pieces of 15-count waste canvas, each measuring (2½ in (6.3 cm) square
1 piece of 15-count waste canvas measuring 6½ in (16.5 cm) square
Contrasting sewing thread for basting
No. 8 crewel needle
Pair of tweezers

DMC 6-strand embroidery floss:

1 skein of yellow (727)
1 skein of blue (340)
1 skein of green (834)
1 skein of dark pink (602)
1 skein of purple (350)
1 skein of medium pink (604)
1 skein of gold (725)
1 skein of lavender (333)
1 skein of green (905)
1 skein of rust (900)
1 skein of light pink (963)

Instructions
Position the four smallest pieces of waste canvas approximately 10 inches (25.4 cm) in from each corner of the tablecloth with the vertical lines on the canvas pointing diagonally toward the corners; baste in place. Center the large piece of waste canvas and baste in place. Mark the center of each piece of waste canvas and the center of the charts. Starting here, work the designs in cross-stitch using two strands of floss over two threads of canvas. When the embroidery is complete, carefully remove the threads of canvas from under the stitching with the tweezers.

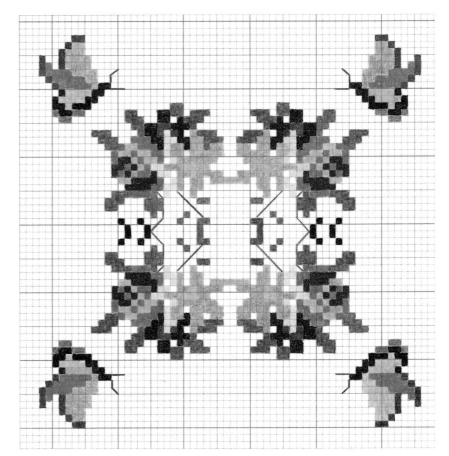

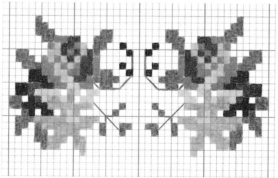

JAPANESE
LIVING ROOM

The imagery and art of Japan has had a profound influence on our lifestyles and our crafts. This influence is interpreted either through the use of exquisite florals with their unique composition of brushstrokes or the stark minimalism of futons, screens, and bold abstract images. Many contemporary homes include a room decorated in an Oriental style.

The impact of Japanese costumes, both traditional and theatrical, comes largely from their richly illustrated embroideries, which often depict flowers and birds. However, for the following projects, I have chosen to use Japanese characters and abstract sunrise motifs to fit in with a contemporary living environment.

Japanese Sunrise Bookmark

This simple design could be adapted to a runner or placemat by using a lower-count fabric. A larger version worked to the same theme would also be effective as a window shade.

Actual design measures:
2¼ × 9 in (5.7 × 22.9 cm)

Materials
1 piece of 32-count linen measuring
  3 × 10½ in (7.5 × 27 cm)
No. 8 crewel needle
1 red bead

DMC 6-strand embroidery floss:

▢ *1 skein of red (606)*

◼ *1 skein of black (310)*

Instructions
Mark the center of the linen and the center of the chart. Starting here, work the design in cross-stitch using two strands of floss over two threads of linen. When the embroidery is complete, take a 6-inch (15.25 cm) length of four strands of black floss and twist them tightly. Fold them in half to form a twisted cord and thread one end through the bead. Knot to secure. Center and stitch the other end to the wrong side of the lower end of the bookmark. Fringe the edges of the linen.

Japanese Paperweight

Blank paperweights provide a useful and interesting showcase for your cross-stitch designs and can be purchased at craft or needlework stores in a variety of shapes and sizes. This round paperweight works particularly well with my Japanese sun as the curved glass emphasizes the shape of the design.

Actual design measures: approximately 2½ in (6.3 cm) square

Materials

1 round paperweight 3½ in (8.9 cm) in diameter (see suppliers information on page 165)
1 piece of 18-count Aida measuring 4 in (10 cm) square
No. 8 crewel needle

DMC 6-strand embroidery floss:

■ *1 skein of black (310)*
▨ *1 skein of red (606)*

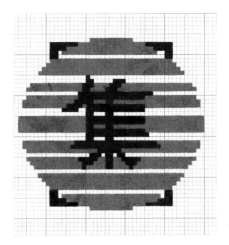

Instructions

Mark the center of the chart and the center of the Aida. Starting here, work in cross-stitch using two strands of floss. When the embroidery is complete, cut into a round using the bottom of the paperweight as a template. Assemble following the manufacturer's instructions.

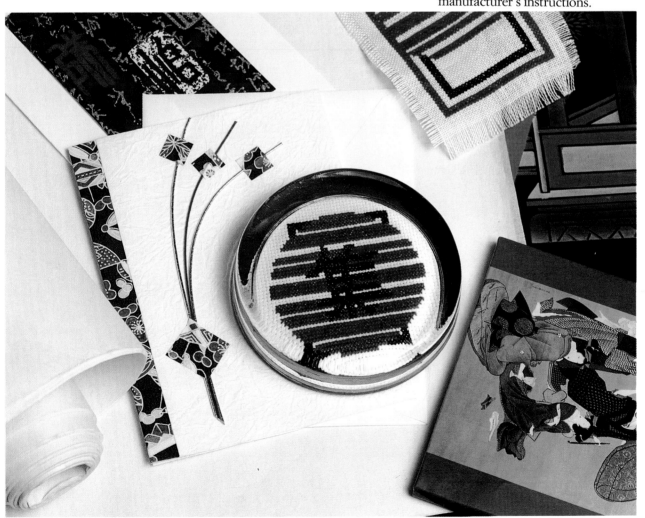

Japanese Address Book

This is the perfect gift for the man who has everything, and it can be adapted to any size address book. Buy the plain book before you begin and cut your cloth accordingly, working the design in the center.

Actual design measures:
4½ × 6¾ in (11.5 × 17.1 cm)

Materials

1 piece of 14-count black Aida measuring 10 × 13 in (25.4 × 33 cm)
2 strips of heavyweight red cotton measuring 3 × 10 in (7.5 × 25.4 cm)
1 address book measuring 5½ × 8 in (14 × 20.5 cm)
Red sewing thread
No. 24 tapestry needle
Fabric glue

DMC 6-strand embroidery floss:

 1 skein of red (606)

 1 skein of white

Instructions

Fold the Aida in half crosswise. Mark the center of the chart and, leaving a 1-inch (2.5-cm) margin on the right-hand edge, center the design on the right-hand side of the Aida (to the right of the fold).

Using two strands of floss, work the design entirely in cross-stitch. When the embroidery is complete, turn under all the edges of the Aida so it fits exactly over the closed address book. Glue the top and bottom hems to the wrong side of the Aida. Take one strip of red cotton fabric and stitch one long edge to the fold on the right-hand edge of the Aida. Fold the red fabric to form a pocket to hold the book cover, then turn under and stitch the top and bottom edges of red fabric to the top and bottom folded edges of the Aida. Repeat for the left side. Slip the address book covers into the pockets.

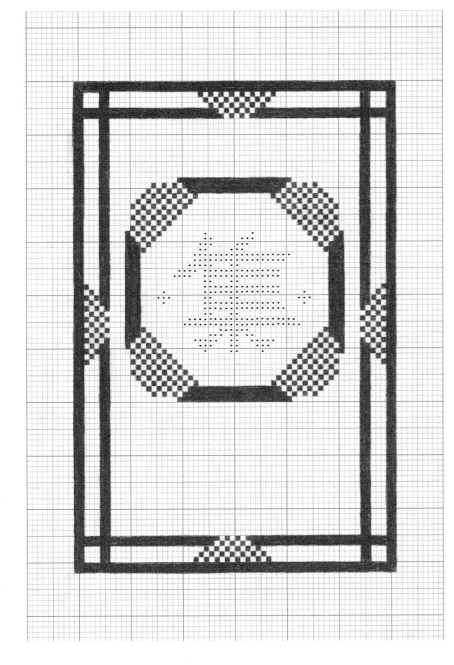

Japanese Lampshade

Fabric lampshades in numerous shapes and sizes can be purchased inexpensively from home stores. When selecting a lampshade for embroidery purposes, check that it doesn't have a stiff cardboard or parchment lining. I would also suggest that you do not attempt to embroider a pleated or gathered shade. Also bear in mind that if you work on a light-colored fine fabric with a dark thread, the back of your stitching may show through when the lamp is turned on. For this reason I have used a lampshade covered in a heavy cotton fabric.

Actual design measures:
3¾ × 5 in (9.5 × 12.7 cm)

Materials
Fabric lampshade
1 piece of 10-count waste canvas
measuring 5 × 6 in
(12.7 × 15.25 cm)
Sewing thread for basting
No. 7 crewel needle

DMC Matte Coton

 2 skeins of black (310)

Instructions
Baste the waste canvas over the portion of the lampshade you wish to embroider. Mark the center of the chart and the center of the waste canvas and work from here using one strand of matte cotton and working in cross-stitch throughout over two threads of canvas. Take care not to carry thread across unworked areas at the back of the lampshade as it will show through when the lamp is turned on.

When the embroidery is complete, carefully remove the strands of waste canvas from under the stitching with a pair of tweezers.

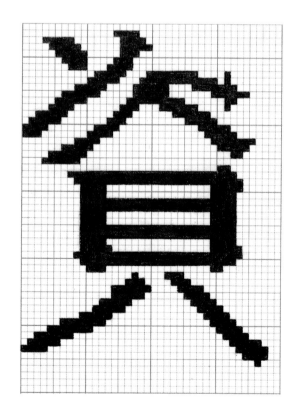

GAME TABLE
LIVING ROOM

Playing cards, dice, Scrabble® tiles, and Monopoly® boards all provide decorative, inspirational images. Here are just a few ideas to liven up an evening of cards, but I am sure that you will find many variations of your own. Embroideries based on favorite games make lovely gifts for enthusiasts, and, if you use this collection of items as a springboard, you could vary it to include favorite hobbies . . . a little bag for golf tees, a folder for cake decorating ideas, key rings, credit card holders, paperweights . . . look around gift stores and in catalogs for ideas — but don't buy them, make them.

Game Tray

Framecraft makes a number of different-sized trays especially designed to display your embroidery. You could embroider a square tray in the image of a game board — chess, backgammon, or perhaps even Scrabble®. If you don't want to buy a tray, why not display your embroidery under the glass top of a coffee table?

Actual design measures:
6½ × 9½ in (16.5 × 24 cm)

Materials

Framecraft tray with oval opening measuring 7¼ × 10¼ in (18.4 × 26.6 cm) (see suppliers on page 165)

1 piece of 14-count Aida measuring 8½ × 12 in (21.6 × 30.5 cm)

No. 24 tapestry needle

DMC 6-strand embroidery floss:

3 skeins of blue (798)

1 skein of red (891)

1 skein of black (310)

1 skein of yellow (725)

Instructions

Mark the center of the chart and the center of the Aida. Starting here, work the design in cross-stitch using three strands of floss. Work the outline of the cards and the oval in black straight stitches using three strands of floss. When the embroidery is complete, mount it in the tray following the manufacturer's instructions.

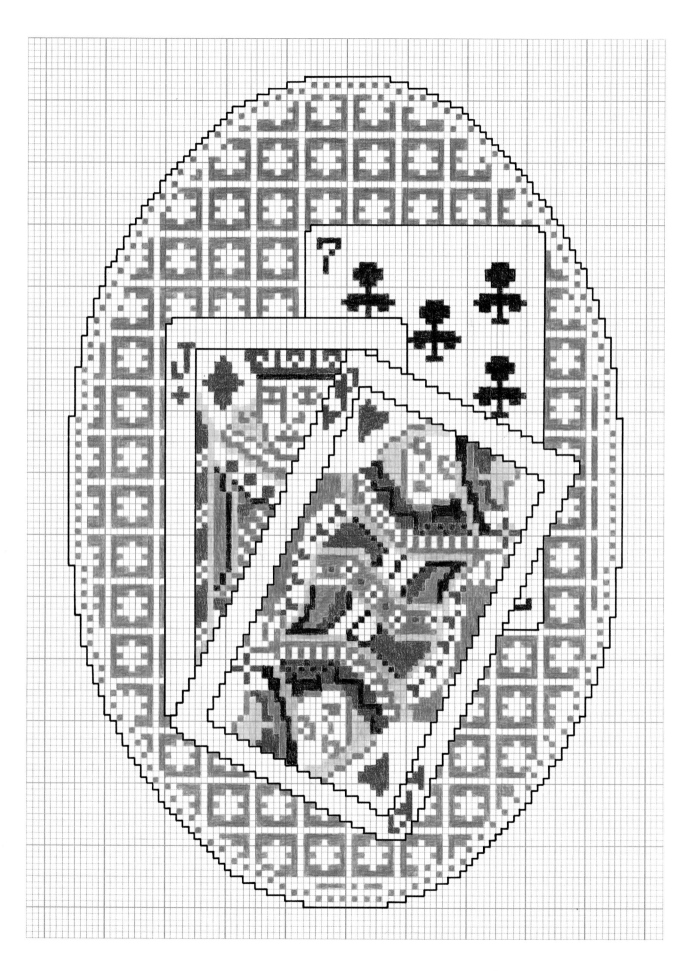

Bridge Pad

This is a neat idea for a bridge pad cover. I have used an ordinary spiral-bound scorepad, mounted the finished embroidery on cardboard and glued it to the front. When the pad is finished, all you need do is tear off the cover and glue it to the front of a new pad.

Actual design measures:
4¾ × 7 in (12 × 17.8 cm)

Materials

1 piece of 11-count Aida measuring
　　7 × 10 in (17.8 × 25.4 cm)
1 spiral-bound scorepad measuring
　　5 × 8 in (12.7 × 20.5 cm)
1 piece of cardboard to fit over the
　　front of the scorepad
No. 23 tapestry needle
Rubber-based adhesive

DMC 6-strand embroidery floss:

1 skein of blue (798)

1 skein of yellow (725)

1 skein of red (891)

1 skein of black (310)

Instructions

Mark the center of the chart and the center of the Aida. Starting here, work in cross-stitch using four strands of floss. Work the outlines as indicated on the chart in straight stitch using three strands of black floss. When the embroidery is complete, center it over the cardboard, wrap and glue the edges of the fabric to the back. Glue the mounted piece directly onto the front of the scorepad.

Playing Card Glasses Case

This project shows how you can reduce or enlarge an image by using fabrics with different thread counts.

Actual design measures:
2¼ × 6½ in (5.7 × 16.5 cm)

Materials

1 piece of 18-count Aida measuring
　　4 × 9 in (10 × 22.9 cm)
1 piece of quilted backing fabric
　　measuring 4 × 9 in
　　(10 × 22.9 cm)
1 piece of black braid ½ in (12 mm)
　　wide and 8 in (20 cm) long
No. 25 tapestry needle
Black sewing thread

DMC 6-strand embroidery floss:

1 skein of blue (798)

1 skein of yellow (725)

1 skein of red (891)

1 skein of black (310)

Instructions

Mark the center of the chart and of the Aida. Starting here, work in cross-stitch using two strands of floss. When the embroidery is complete, fold under and baste the edges, leaving a ½-inch (12-mm) border of Aida around the design. Place the quilted fabric wrong side up. Fold the edges up so you will have a ¼-inch (6-mm) border of fabric visible around all the edges of the Aida; baste. Stitch the Aida to the quilted fabric, leaving one end open. Hand stitch the braid around the open end.

Card Motif Coaster Set

Coasters and paperweights are ideal for cross-stitch and can be purchased specially made to display stitchery (see the suppliers on page 165). Alternatively, you can make up your own using glass or Pyrex® saucers. Here is how it is done:

Actual design measures:
2½ in (6.3 cm) in diameter

DMC 6-strand embroidery floss:

 2 skeins of blue (798)

 1 skein of red (891)

 1 skein of black (310)

Materials

4 glass coasters or saucers with 3-in (7.5-cm) diameter bases
4 circles of cardboard the same size as the coaster bases
4 circles of self-adhesive felt slightly larger than the coaster bases
4 pieces of 18-count Aida measuring 4 in (10 cm) square
No. 25 tapestry needle
Rubber-based adhesive
Craft knife

Instructions

Mark the center of the charts and the center of each piece of Aida. Starting here, work in cross-stitch using two strands of floss until the embroidery is complete. Center a circle of cardboard over each embroidery, mark around the edge, and cut the Aida on the marked lines. Peel the paper backing off the circles of felt and press one onto the wrong side of each piece of embroidery. Then press the remaining sticky edges of the felt to the bottom of the coasters.

Note: If you cannot find self-adhesive felt, buy the clear self-adhesive acetate used for covering books and secure your design to the coaster with this. Kits are available for the coasters and come complete with felt and cardboard (see suppliers information on page 165).

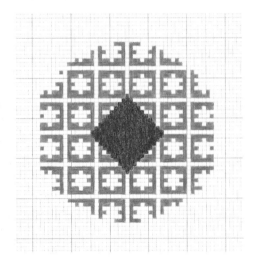

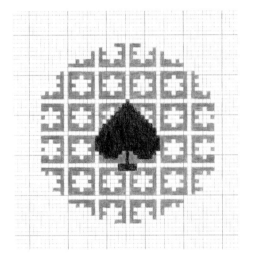

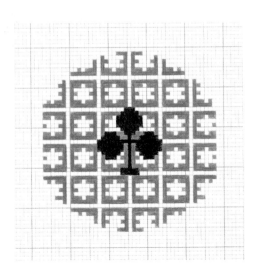

TECHNIQUES

Cross-stitch should be a relaxing and therapeutic pastime. For this reason I have no intention of challenging you with complicated instructions or baffling you with difficult finishing techniques. The object of the exercise is simply to achieve a neatly worked piece of embroidery without bumps and blemishes and to make sure that all your top stitches slant in the same direction. I have indicated alongside the various projects my own approach to finishing the specific items. However, there are many other ways of achieving the same results, and it really doesn't matter what route you take as long as you are happy with your finished piece.

The information in this section will introduce you to the variety of materials and techniques that you can use in order to transform your design into something special. These materials and guidelines are tried and tested and will give you the means to produce professionally finished work of which you can be proud.

Material Facts

The first thing you must decide is what fabric you are going to stitch on. This will be dictated by the size and purpose of your finished item, the intricacy of the design, and your chosen threads. I have listed here a selection of traditional needlework fabrics, all of which should be available in any good needlecaft shop.

Evenweave fabrics

Needlecraft stores stock a wide range of what are known as evenweave fabrics. "Evenweave" means that there are the same number of horizontal and vertical threads in the material, making it easy to count the threads and to make your stitches a uniform size. You will select your fabric according to the count which is, in this case, determined by the number of threads you work your cross-stitch over.

For example, for fine work you would choose a fabric with a high count and work over one or two threads, while for a bold pattern you would choose a coarser fabric. Throughout the text in this book, I have referred to the measurement of the fabric as "count," which refers to the number of threads per inch. Place your tape measure on a vertical thread of fabric and count how many intersecting threads there are in 1 inch. Hardanger and Linda are both higher-count evenweave fabrics that can be bought from good needlework stores.

Basketweave fabrics

These are particularly easy to work on because the holes into which you stitch are clearly defined and you stitch over the intersection of only one horizontal and one vertical thread. These are great for beginners. In this category I would

recommend Aida or Herta. These are brand names for basketweave fabrics that are available in a range of different counts (threads per inch), and will enable you to produce a bold, striking pattern or delicate, intricate design with relative ease. The count you select will determine the size of your finished embroidery and will also dictate the thickness of the thread that you can use. The lower the count of the fabric, the fewer stitches per inch it will produce. Herta is widely used in schools and for children's projects because the count is about 6 stitches per inch and it is available in a good range of bright colors. Aida is usually available in 10–18 count in a subtler range of colors.

Embroidery linens

These are available in high counts and provide a sophisticated background for your work. However, they are expensive, so before selecting them give consideration to your eyesight and the time available to you. If you

have owlish vision and endless time on your hands, you can even produce cross-stitch miniatures by working on silk gauze. This can be purchased pre-mounted in a frame, but it really needs to be worked through a magnifying glass: eat lots of carrots before beginning.

Perforated paper

This is a traditional medium which reached its height in popularity during the Victorian era. It is currently enjoying a revival among stitchers and is used for simple cutout projects (see Cupid Mirror) and items such as greeting cards, bookmarks, and Christmas decorations.

Special embroidery fabrics

These are usually sold by the yard, although you will often require only a very small piece for a project such as a greeting card. For this reason, many needlecraft shops sell bags of scraps, which can be good value.

In addition to traditional fabrics, manufacturers are now extending their ranges to include damasks with inserted panels ready for you to embroider. You can also find special Aida and linen borders to embroider and stitch onto towels, bedspreads, etc.

What you will

Any fabric store will offer a range of materials on which to embroider designs, but most sewing fabrics have an irregular weave or are too fine to count. With a little experience you can safely select cottons with regular patterning such as stripes, ginghams, and damasks and gauge your stitch positions according to the pattern. Do not attempt to use stretch or knitted fabrics — your work may pucker. Be sure thread size and fabric are compatible.

Waste not

Waste canvas is a miraculous fabric that makes it possible to cross-stitch on almost any fabric. It is basically a very loosely woven canvas that is available in a selection of counts. To use it, baste it to the fabric you wish to embellish. It will form an instant grid that defines the size and position of your stitches in the same manner as an evenweave fabric. Cross-stitch your design in the usual way and then pull out the threads of waste canvas from under your stitching with the help of a pair of tweezers. If you pull out all the vertical threads first, you will find that the horizontal threads virtually fall away by themselves. If you have any problems removing these threads, dampen the fabric and you will find they are easier to remove.

Thread Up

While I have specified particular embroidery thread color numbers, your finished project will not be ruined if you go up or down a shade. Floss goes a long way,

especially if you are working on a high content fabric so, after cross-stitching for just a short time, you are bound to build up a useful collection of half-used skeins that can be incorporated into future projects.

There is a vast array of threads on the market, and your choice will add to the individuality of your work. I have listed a selection of these below and leave it to you to experiment with the different effects and highlights you can achieve. A major consideration should be that all the threads you use in a single project should be of the same thickness. If you mix thicknesses, you will end up with some skimpy crosses and some fat ones, which will not be a pretty sight — unless of course, you intend them to look that way.

6-strand embroidery floss

These are sold in small skeins of 8 meters (approximately 26 feet) containing six individual strands loosely twisted together. To use them, cut a workable length — about 20 inches — and separate the strands so that you have as many as you need for your particular fabric, or as specified in the project directions. You can of course mix strands of several colors together to give a subtle shaded effect, and you can buy skeins that are already shaded.

Matte Cotton

This is a flat unmercerized thread which works well in bolder designs. It comes in a good choice of colors, but does pick up dust more easily than the slightly shiny mercerized varieties. Danish and German flower threads are also flat cotton threads, but are finer. All are spun as a single ply and are not designed to be separated or stranded. They impart a lovely soft quality to your work.

Silks

Embroidery floss is mercerized and therefore has a pleasantly silky luster. However, for the perfectionists among us, there is nothing like the real thing. Silk is available in stranded form and in twisted threads. It is expensive and not very easy to work with because the delicate fibers snag on rough skin. However, the finished effect on very fine work is quite special . . . reserve it for your masterpiece.

Pearl cottons

Pearl cotton (coton perlé) is a single-twist, high-luster thread that comes in a good selection of colors, including some with a shaded effect. It is available in three different weights, which you use as is appropriate for your fabric.

Novelty threads

In addition to the above, novelty threads, including a wonderful range of metallics by Kreinik, are constantly being introduced. These can be used to great effect for highlighting details, but be sure to check that the thickness of the thread is consistent with the other threads you have chosen.

Get Organized

If you are anything like me, you will always pull the wrong loose end on a skein of thread and end up with a knotted mess that will prove a great joy to your cat. To avoid this, it is a good idea to make yourself a thread organizer before beginning a project. All you need is a small strip of lightweight cardboard (an old greeting card is ideal) and a hole punch. Make a hole for each color down the right-hand side of the card and cut your thread into manageable lengths — 20 inches is fine. Next to the relevant hole, write the color number and, if appropriate, the symbol on the chart, and loop your lengths of thread through it. You can then easily pull out the thread as and when you need it.

Get the Needle

To work cross-stitch on evenweave fabrics, use a blunt-ended tapestry needle. To work using waste canvas you need a selection of crewel needles with sharp points and long, flat eyes that allow you to thread a number of strands through at one time without damaging the fabric.

Needles are available in various sizes, and the size you use will depend on the fabric count and the number of strands you are using. A suggested size is given with each project but, as a rule of thumb, use one that feels comfortable and travels easily through your fabric.

Embroidery Frames

When I am working with an evenweave fabric such as Aida, I do not consider it necessary to use a frame. However, I always use a frame when I am stitching on non-evenweave fabrics or working on a very large project.

There are various types of frames

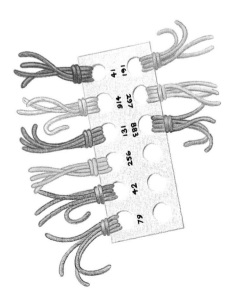

A thread organizer.

on the market, and the most popular for cross-stitch is the hoop, which consists of two concentric circles, one of which is laid under your work and the other laid over your work and then tightened with a screw to hold the fabric taut. It is a good idea to bind both rings with woven tape before beginning because the hoop may mark or distort delicate fabrics. Never leave a hoop on your fabric when you are not stitching.

The other most popular type of frame consists of two parallel dowels with webbing onto which you baste the opposite ends of your fabric. The dowels are then slotted into two straight uprights, which can be tightened to hold them securely. You can rotate the dowels to move the fabric up and down and to keep it taut.

Light Up

One miracle of modern science that I would not be without is the daylight bulb. Given that most of us are busy people who only have the evenings available to stitch in, good lighting, especially when you are counting stitches, is essential. Daylight bulbs ease the strain and can be combined with a custom-made magnifying lamp on an adjustable stand, all of which makes stitching comfortable and pleasurable. (See the suppliers information on page 165). You can also buy special holders for your charts and no end of other paraphernalia that will help you to get the job done and take the strain out of your work.

Charts

Many people are frightened of charts, but all you need to remember is that every colored square represents one complete cross-stitch. The heavier lines on the grid are put there to make

counting stitches easier. Each block of squares between the heavy lines represents 10 stitches. The color key is coded to the thread by number so you really cannot go wrong. I work in blocks of color rather than rows, and I keep a number of needles threaded with the different colors of thread so I can change from one to another as necessary.

Sizing the Design

For almost every design in this book, I give the actual size of the motif that you will make if you work on my recommended background fabric. However, it is quite easy to re-size the motif by changing the count of the fabric you use. There is a simple formula for working out the size of your design — let's take the game tray design as an example. First, count the number of stitches across at the widest point; on this chart it is 92 stitches. Now count the number of stitches vertically; it is 134. If you were going to work this design on 28-count linen over two threads, you would need to halve the count to determine the number of stitches to the inch; in other words, on 28-count linen you would actually have 14 stitches to the inch. You should now divide the number of stitches on your chart by the number of stitches to the inch — that is (width) 92 stitches divided by 14 = 6.57 inches × (height) 134 stitches divided by 14 = 9.57 inches. (When you are working on Aida, or over one thread of fabric, do not halve the count before dividing.)

When calculating how much fabric you need, remember to add at least 3 inches of extra fabric on all sides of each project to fit into a hoop, or for finishing allowances.

If you want to re-size a design in

a major way, your best approach is with a hand-drawn grid. First, trace the outline of your design and draw a squared grid over it. Draw a second grid to the size you require and copy the design square by square from one to the other. Place the enlarged version over a sheet of graph paper and fill in the symbols within the traced outlines. This approach should also be used when copying designs from fabric or china (see the Mix-and-Match section). Alternatively, you can enlarge your design with the use of a photocopier.

Charting paper is now available in clear acetate, which you can place over any image that you wish to chart and fill in with symbols.

Another method of enlarging is to read every symbol on the chart as a block of four stitches. This in principle will double the size of your design, although you may find it necessary to round off corners by omitting or adding a few stitches at the edges as you work.

Transferring Designs

If you do not wish to work with waste canvas, you can easily transfer the image with a water-erasable transfer pencil (available from needlework and craft stores) and tracing paper. First, test your fabric by drawing a cross on the tracing paper. Place this face down on the fabric and press it with a warm iron. If it transfers to the fabric, you can then trace and transfer your complete design. There are some wonderful color transfer pens and paints on the market, so you could trace or paint the design in full color and then transfer it to the fabric.

Centering Designs

Throughout the book I have suggested that you find the center of the fabric before beginning your embroidery. There are various methods of doing this. If you are using Aida, you can count the threads vertically and horizontally and halve the totals to find the center. You could use a tape measure and halve the measurement, or you can fold the fabric both horizontally and vertically to establish the center point. When you are establishing the center point on a piece of fabric that has a selvage on one side, be sure to start your count or measurement on the evenweave area.

To find the center of the charts, count the squares and halve the total. If there is no stitch at the center point, count out to the nearest stitch and start on the equivalent position on your fabric. On establishing your central point, you might find it useful to baste a line of sewing thread both horizontally and vertically on your fabric as a guide. Always work out from the center unless the instructions specify otherwise.

Getting Started

Before beginning your work, prevent potential disasters by making sure of the following:

1 Your hands are spotlessly clean. They will need regular washing as fabrics and threads pick up dirt very easily.

2 Your tea or coffee is at a safe distance from your work and that delicious chocolate cake with the gooey icing is not sitting there tempting you to pick it up.

3 The animals have all been instructed not to sit on your lap/ shoulder/head and have learned to wipe their paws before coming in from the garden and climbing all over you.

4 The children are doing their

Cross-stitch on plainweave fabric.

Cross-stitch on basketweave fabric (Aida).

painting somewhere else.

5 No one or nothing within reach of you is molting.

Stitching

Remember the first rule of cross-stitch — that all the top stitches slant in the same direction. This can be achieved either by working a row of bottom stitches in one direction and then coming back along the row in the opposite direction or by working each complete cross individually. Both these methods are perfectly acceptable, but the option you choose will depend on how many stitches you have in a row before the color changes. You can work in any direction, but always insert your needle after the correct number of threads in your background material. The diagrams show a cross-stitch being worked over two threads on a simple evenweave fabric and on a basketweave fabric such as Aida. It is a good idea to thread several needles with different colors before you begin. Use a needle threader — it will save your sight and a great deal of time.

Cross-stitch is the only stitch you need to master to complete the majority of projects in this book.

However, one or two of the designs require additional stitches. When I refer to straight stitch, I mean exactly that: small backstitches worked in a row, the same size as a half cross-stitch. Half stitch is as it sounds, work the first half of a cross-stitch only, i.e. do not go back to complete the full cross. I have also used star stitch on the Shell Make-up Bag (see page 80).

Stretching

I did not find it necessary to block any of the projects in this book. However, if you do find the shape of your work is slightly distorted, place it face down on a piece of cardboard, which you should cover with clean paper or a sheet, and pull it into shape by inserting tacks at 1 inch intervals. Dampen your work with a clean sponge or spray, and leave it to dry.

Framing

Because cross-stitch fabric is very soft, it is usually quite simple when you are framing projects to stretch your finished work into shape on a backing board and either glue it into position using a rubber-based adhesive or fabric glue or, using heavy thread, lace it across the back

in crisscross fashion until it is taut (see diagram). Before using either of these methods, center your finished work on your cardboard and insert pins, starting with the four corners and then spaced at 1 inch intervals all around the edge of the needlework and card to make sure it is straight and undistorted. When mounting a piece of embroidery, use acid-free board to make sure it remains in good condition for the generations ahead of you who will treasure your work. You can add a decorative mat to the front or frame it in whichever fashion you please. Finished pieces intended for book covers and folders can be pulled into shape during the finishing process.

Trimmings

I hope this book has given you lots of new ideas for ways to use your cross-stitch projects. Most craftspeople are, by nature, collectors, and I would expect you to have a basket or box of fabric pieces and furnishing trims. Use whatever you fancy to make a project, but consider the weight of any fabric you intend using to be sure it is compatible with the fabric

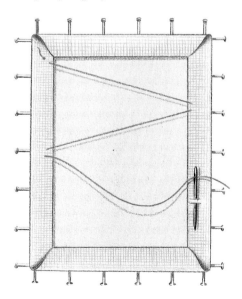

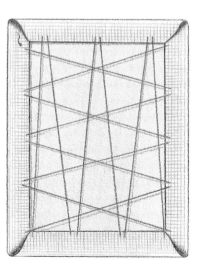

To frame your cross-stitch, center your finished work on a sheet of cardboard and insert pins all the way around at 1 inch intervals. Then either glue into position or lace it across the back with heavy thread, as shown here.

MAKING A CROCHET CHAIN

1 Make a loop

2 Hook yarn through loop

3 Form a slip knot

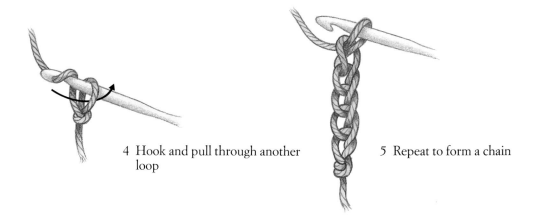

4 Hook and pull through another
loop

5 Repeat to form a chain

you have cross-stitched on. In a couple of projects I have used twisted cords and crochet chains as edgings and fastenings.

To make a twisted cord, hold several strands of floss together and tie one end to a doorknob. Repeatedly twist this length of thread until it is tight and then, keeping it taut, unfasten the tied end. Hold both ends together and let the doubled cord twist around itself. Secure at both ends.

To make a crochet chain, follow the step-by-step diagrams above.

Care

However careful you are, accidents inevitably happen. If you have used the recommended threads, you should have no problem repairing the damage. Before washing a piece of embroidery always check the colorfastness of the thread and fabric you have used and follow the manufacturer's instructions. Most embroidery threads are reputed to

be colorfast and can be machine washed at 96°F but you must also take the instructions for washing the background fabric into account. As a general rule, avoid bleach and biological powders and do not tumble dry. When you iron your work, place it face down over a fluffy towel to prevent any flattening of the stitches. Then steam press or use a damp cloth, ironing on the wrong side of the work only.

Suppliers Information

Many of the lace and cotton items featured in this book are available as complete embroidery kits by mail order. For full details contact the following:

Essentially British Ltd.
P.O. Box 547
Dove, MA 02030

If items mentioned in the book cannot be found in your area, contact the following businesses for a local supplier:

For Candle Screen, page 100; Collector's Cabinet, page 91; Paperweight, page 145; Game Tray, page 152; Coasters, page 156; Brush, Mirror and Comb Set, page 99; Linen Towel, page 103; Door Plate, page 164; Bellpull, page 136; Grow Chart Fixtures, page 56.

Ann Brinkley Designs
761 Palmer Avenue
Holmdel, NJ 97733

Gay Bowles Sales Inc.
P.O. Box 1060
Janesville, WI 53547

For floss:

Coats & Clark (Anchor®) Inc.
P.O. Box 27067
Department C01
Greenville, SC 29615

The DMC Corporation
American Needlewoman 1-800-433-2231
Herrschner's 1-800-441-0838

For metallic floss:

Kreinik Manufacturing Co. Inc.
1-800-537-2166

For needlework fabrics and some prefinished items:

Charles Craft Inc.
P.O. Box 1049
Laurinburg, NC 28353-1049

Needleworker's Delight (Zweigart Fabrics)
214 Marshall Street
Elizabeth, NJ 07206

For ribbons:

Offray Ribbons
360 Rt. 24
Chester, NJ 07930

Conversion Chart									
DMC	Anchor	*DMC*	Anchor	*DMC*	Anchor	*DMC*	Anchor	*DMC*	Anchor
White	1	*451*	233	*727*	293	*892*	28	*3340*	330
(blanc)		*453*	231	*730*	681	*893*	27	*3347*	266
210	109	*518*	168	*741*	304	*894*	26	*3348*	265
223	894	*519*	167	*743*	305	*900*	326	*3609*	85
224	893	*550*	101	*746*	386	*905*	258	*3687*	77
225	892	*552*	99	*754*	4146	*906*	256	*3708*	25
310	403	*553*	97	*762*	397	*907*	255	*3752*	849
326	19	*602*	57	*776*	24	*912*	205	*3761*	928
333	119	*604*	55	*798*	131	*954*	203	*3779*	868
340	118	*606*	334	*800*	128	*956*	54		
341	117	*611*	903	*809*	130	*963*	23		
351	10	*632*	936	*817*	13	*970*	925		
414	235	*699*	229	*827*	159	*995*	410		
415	398	*701*	227	*834*	279	*3051*	861		
437	362	*718*	89	*841*	374	*3053*	843		
444	291	*725*	298	*891*	29	*3078*	292		

Acknowledgements

The author would like to provide all
the following people with luxury
cruises, diamond tiaras, crates of
champagne, and cases of caviar.
As she currently has prior obligations
relating to the feeding of her cats,
chickens, and poodle, she hopes her
sincerest thanks will be enough.

For making this book possible
through their excellent and
endless stitching:
Coral Gibson,
Carolyn Palmer,
Anne Peterson,
Valerie Clark,
Freda Brown, and
Audrey Bonnaud.

For turning the needlework into
lovely things:
Jeanette Hall.

For exceeding herself, yet again,
with her wonderful photography:
Di Lewis.

For nervous breakdown prevention,
my editors:
Jane Donovan and
Jane Struthers.

For encouragement and support:
Carey Smith and
Colin Gower.

For their help and friendship:
Pat Groves and
Lydia Darbyshire.

The publishers would like to thank the following for their kind help in
loaning objects for photography:
Ray Coggins Antiques, Westbury, Wiltshire.
David Plagerson, Totnes, Devon.
Fosse Farmhouse, Nettleford, Near Chippenham, Wiltshire.

Index